*Financial Integration
in Western Europe*

Financial Integration in Western Europe

By ETIENNE-SADI KIRSCHEN

with the collaboration

of HENRY SIMON BLOCH *and*

WILLIAM BRUCE BASSETT

1969

COLUMBIA UNIVERSITY PRESS

NEW YORK & LONDON

Etienne-Sadi Kirschen is Professor of Economics and Director of the Institute of Applied Economics of the Université Libre de Bruxelles.

Henry Simon Bloch is a Professor in the School of International Affairs of Columbia University and a Director of E. M. Warburg & Company, Inc.

William Bruce Bassett is a Professor in the Graduate School of Business of Columbia University.

FOREWORD

THE School of International Affairs of Columbia University over the past few years has sponsored several studies on the subject of economic integration. The interest of the School focuses essentially on the political significance of regional arrangements, but while there have been very numerous investigations into various aspects of European economic integration, relatively little has been written on financial integration, although there were notable studies of European capital markets published by Claudio Segre and the Atlantic Institute.

The School, therefore, requested Professor Etienne S. Kirschen, Director of DULBEA, the Institute of Applied Economics of the Université Libre de Bruxelles, to collaborate with it in an analysis of the specific problems of financial integration.

Professor Kirschen's study deals with harmonization of national policies, liberalization of capital flows, and the problems of institution building in the fields of money, banking, and securities exchanges. We were particularly interested in finding out to what extent systems of government were responsible for difficulties encountered in attaining financial integration, and political and administrative objectives conflicted with economic objectives.

Professor Kirschen is the author of several books on economics and has pioneered in model building for the Belgian and European economy. His Institute has achieved a leading role in its field and he has been called upon to serve on United Nations expert committees. Professor Kirschen has delivered a number of lectures at the School of International Affairs, testing his own ideas with both faculty and students.

Etienne Kirschen is a truly inter-disciplinary person: he has a doctorate in economics from the Université Libre de Bruxelles, was admitted as a professional engineer and chartered accountant in Belgium, and for three years has been serving as President of the faculties of economics, sociology, and political science of his University.

The concept of the present study was originally developed by Professor Henry S. Bloch of the Faculty of International Affairs of Columbia University, who presented it to Professor Kirschen during one of his frequent trips to Belgium. It was further developed by Professor Kirschen during his visit to Columbia University in 1966, in collaboration with Professor Bloch and Professor W. Bruce Bassett of the Graduate School of Business. It might be pointed out that Professors Bloch and Bassett are preparing a book on regional development financing, to be published in 1969. Professor Bassett originally served as senior research assistant to Professor Bloch until his appointment to the faculty in 1967, and devoted most of his time to the study of regional financing.

Professor Kirschen enjoyed the collaboration of Professors Bloch and Bassett throughout the study. Miss Judith Lourie, a Columbia graduate, contributed to the book her special knowledge as translator.

The project in fact is a joint venture of the School of International Affairs of Columbia University and of the Institute of Applied Economics of the Université Libre de Bruxelles.

ANDREW W. CORDIER

INTRODUCTION AND CONCLUSIONS

HOW CAN the fragmented financial structure of the Common Market be integrated? What are the objectives? What are the existing and available instruments, what are the present and potential institutions? While searching for answers to these questions Professor Kirschen decided to omit the usual and oft-repeated catalogue of sins attributed to the United States and the United Kingdom, because at this point their actions have little direct impact upon the financial integration of Europe. In the final analysis, the answers to the pertinent questions depend upon the political will within the Common Market. The governments of the Six must face some basic political decisions and must deal with vested interests impeding rapid financial integration.

Translation of national political goals into economically measurable objectives is not always possible, but an approximation has been made within the Common Market community, as demonstrated in this book. Such objectives fall into the major short-term categories of full employment, price stability, accumulation of foreign exchange and gold reserves, and expansion or growth policy.

The instruments whereby a government approaches these objectives can be divided broadly into three categories: fiscal tools, monetary and credit tools, and qualitative or structural reforms.

Fiscal tools include the public finance aspects of government expenditures and government income; monetary and credit tools encompass the rates of exchange, interest rates, and installment and margin controls. Qualitative or structural reforms are changes of the system itself, as opposed to changes within the system; examples are the introduction of the tax on value added, agreement on a medium-term economic policy throughout the community, and revision of company laws.

Although governments are goaded by national political factors to use these tools for the attainment of particular goals, these instruments cannot be employed without an appraisal of resultant international effects. Unilateral use can set off international repercussions that could lead to internecine retaliations.

To assess the implications of financial integration, the overall philosophy of the Rome Treaty is recalled with its three-pronged approach: the removal of all obstacles to international trade and investment between Common Market countries; the creation of new institutions; and, of course, the harmonization of national economic policies. The Rome Treaty calls for more than just the elimination of customs and trade barriers; it sets a more ambitious goal—economic union—which includes unrestricted movement of capital and labor, freedom of establishment, and common policies for economic development. The free movement of nonagricultural and agricultural goods is explained and acknowledged as a success, as is the agreement to apply a common tariff on goods coming from third countries. The half-success of antitrust regulation is recognized, while the list of failures is highlighted by very weak common transport and social policies and, above all, by the almost total lack of a common energy policy.

Professor Kirschen quotes extensively from Spaak's Messina Report, not widely known in the United States, and he relies also on Claudio Segre's brilliant interpretations of Community policies. Precisely on this matter, it is worth noting that Segre believes that the authorities of the Community should be given the responsibility of defining and executing the economic policies regarding short-term objectives. Under this system the Common Market could prohibit, and/or compensate for, inappropriate uses of policy instruments by member states. The implementation of anticyclical trade policy measures to reach objectives set by the Community authorities, however, would be left to individual governments.

Community harmonization of policies is much more vague in practice, and much less well defined in the Treaty of Rome, than is generally believed. Peculiar difficulty resides in attaining an overall approach to *all* major instruments and in coordinating the use of these instruments for unified objectives. Moreover, additional complexities arise from the absence of a will for collaboration between very strong national institutions, such as central banks and sometimes ministries of finance and national economy.

Some instruments are controlled by the Community authorities, for example, quantitative restrictions on private imports and exports, customs duties, exchange controls, and subsidies to business. The Common Market authorities influence furthermore, the conditions of competition.

National governments still control a number of instruments that must be harmonized, especially indirect taxes on internal transactions. The most dramatic step toward harmonization has been the agreement to extend the value-added tax system to all six member countries by 1970. This frequently misinterpreted tax is designed to provide a more sophisticated indirect instrument than the other forms of sales and turnover taxes, which generally promoted vertical integration to escape multiple taxation and discouraged specialization. As other barriers and differences in competitive conditions between member states are eliminated, the rates of the value-added tax will have to be harmonized. The same is true of some direct taxes, although the Rome Treaty does not refer to their harmonization. Without harmonization of direct taxes on business profits, movements of capital within the community and choices of plant locations will be unduly influenced by tax considerations. There is also need for harmonization of taxes on financial transactions, such as stock exchange transactions. Exchange rate policy is harmonized to a degree, but central bank discount rates are not always coordinated.

Other instruments used by national governments with little harmonization include loans and guarantees to business, control of private business borrowing, control of bank credit, and control of credit by nonbank financial institutions. There has been no community alignment of controls over access to national capital markets and stock exchanges. Company laws and other laws affecting business institutions are also under the control of national governments, and no joint approach has been effectively made.

The Spaak Report emphasized the need for liberalizing capital flows, and a procedure is set forth in the Rome Treaty. Present obstacles to the liberalization procedure raise issues that are delineated in this book in full statistical and legal terms. The obstacles to European capital flows include the difficulties of dividend control, access to capital markets, especially stock exchanges, and the continuing tax differentials. Increased liberalization will require a great deal of nongovernmental action. European enterprises should make more disclosures, institutional investors should be more flexible in their policies, stock exchanges should rationalize themselves, and European banks that complain about U.S. incursion into their markets can expand their own European operations. There was not a single major commercial bank merger beyond national frontiers within the Common Market during the first decade of its existence. This, however, may change during the second decade. The not widely known, yet increasingly significant, interlocking ownership of European banks and, much more important, of their subsidiaries, such as those created in Luxembourg for international financial activities, are a crucial factor inhibiting rationalizations by the merger route.

Although there is not yet a European market for shares, one is emerging for debentures. The Eurodollar market and the smaller "unit of account" market are well known, yet they must be placed in context to give an overview of the various modalities of Euroloans as well as of the legal and institutional positions regarding intra-European capital flows. This method serves a didactic purpose, especially as synoptic tables facilitate illumination of the otherwise complex problems.

Distinguishing liberalization from harmonization provides a useful analytical approach to the problems of European financial integration. However, the distinction should not cloud the fact that in many areas liberalization requires harmonization and, consequently, that there are often problems common to both of these approaches. For instance, in connection with the analysis of international tax harmonization it is pointed out that many governments do not like to alter bilateral tax treaties reached with governments outside the Six—a noneconomic but understandable inclination. Without alteration of such treaties, harmonization within the Six is handicapped.

Harmonization and liberalization of European finance may or may not be facilitated through the creation of new institutions. The European Investment Bank, operating since 1958, has never been a strong force for improvements in the mobilization and channeling of capital within the Community. It is strong, however, in the associated developing nations of Europe and overseas. In the late fifties and early sixties, an example of integrating strength on a supranational level was given by the European Coal and Steel Community, whose High Authority, backed by powers of taxation and regulation, proved to be an able borrower and lender. When difficulties arose in the coal sector during the late sixties, however, nationalistic tendencies resulting from social and political pressures caused a decline in the effectiveness of the High Authority. The merger of Community organs, which began in July 1967, places the High Authority in a new role that has not yet been tested.

Widening markets, accelerating technological progress, and sharpening international competition are pressuring European companies to expand their operations. The American business challenge has convinced Europeans of the necessity for more broadly based operations which can, among other benefits, narrow the technological gap by financing more industrial research and development, attract better management personnel and techniques, and capitalize on potential economies of scale.

In many cases expansion could best be accomplished through the merger route. However, this would often result in mergers between companies from different countries within the Community; although these mergers would certainly promote European financial integration, the governments involved are reluctant to lose control over their nationally chartered, revenue-producing corporations. Consequently, international mergers have not been encouraged. In all member countries except the Netherlands, mergers between companies of Common Market members entail the winding up of the firm being absorbed and the payment of a capital gains tax on the difference between the actual and the book value of the company's assets. New approaches are now being developed, and especially France and the Federal Republic of Germany are interested in joint private enterprises.

A great challenge lies in the creation of a European company charter, which could be either a supranational company whose juridical existence would be based upon a transnational enabling statute or, as the French propose, a European company enjoying equal legal status throughout the Common Market. The French assume uniform legislation, which would have to be enacted by each country on its own. Companies would then incorporate by using either a national or a European charter. So much conflict has arisen over the theoretical legal framework and the working hypotheses, however, that, regrettably, there is not even conceptual agreement among Common Market governments concerning this important facet of European financial integration.

This book provides a framework which will enable the observer to follow the process of financial integration in the Common

Market and to better understand the issues as they arise. The statistical comparisons have been chosen to best illustrate the comparative setting of the process. To provide a better historical perspective, 1964 was selected as a benchmark year.

Let us now conclude. The Six suffer from the absence of indigenous multinational private financial institutions. It cannot be emphasized enough that Common Market commercial and investment banks have considerable weaknesses, which prevent their effective collaboration even within the Common Market itself. Into this breach have stepped American commercial banks, whose networks of branches, joint ventures, representatives, and correspondents have facilitated a remarkable degree of financial integration, especially through the Eurodollar market. In the European capital markets American and English investment bankers have taken the lead in forming and managing large European underwriting syndicates. Though these placements have been in significant amounts, they do not reflect a meaningful increase in intra-Community capital flows because most of the investment proceeds originate outside the Common Market. What is of importance in regard to both the networks of American commercial banks and the international underwriting syndicates is the competitive effect on financial institutions within the Six. As these local institutions respond to the opportunities demonstrated by American and English bankers, they will become more positive forces behind European financial integration. Already, European banks are beginning to insist on an active role in the formation and management of underwriting syndicates.

European financial institutions are at a competitive disadvantage in their parochial settings. The reform of securities exchanges proceeds at a slow pace, and the national capital markets are certainly not as well developed as is even the British capital market. Industrial organization has not yet progressed to such a degree as to offer the investment vehicles that American companies are offering, and even the best-organized European capital markets will not have available enough top-grade European industrial issues to displace the very strong convertible obligations of major American companies unless administrative restrictions, which further impede European financial integration, are applied.

Entry of Britain into the Common Market in the next decade is possible. The devaluation of the pound in November 1967 removed one of the obstacles to entry; however, liquidation of the sterling area is a remaining prerequisite that will be more difficult to accomplish.

British entry will bring greater technology and management expertise, thus giving the Common Market many more top-grade industrial issues to compete with those of American companies. In addition, British entry will introduce new private financial thinking with a world-wide perspective. With Britain in the Common Market, the powerful voice of British banking will be heard urging rapid financial integration.

It must be emphasized that without a monetary system for Europe, without a European central bank, the institutional prerequisites for an effective regional capital market do not exist. There is also no regional development bank of sufficient size and freedom of action; the European Investment Bank, the "Bank of the Common Market," is too limited by its statutes and too small in size to serve as an effective financial institution for the Six. In spite of very great progress in commercial, agricultural, and even industrial regionalization, Europe has remained weak as a capital market and will remain weak for some time to come, unless major structural reforms take place in both the private and public sectors.

To the world, in its formal declarations, the European Economic Community speaks as a unit. The central bankers rarely talk out of turn, although different trends of thinking are known to exist among them. In France there has been a barrage of public policy declarations at the political summit, and little is heard from the central bank.

Some of the French actions, too (e.g., the gold pool participation), have not been in line with those of the other Common Market countries, but the true difference is a doctrinal one, a difference in objectives, with France attempting to reach for national monetary strength by attacking the dollar as the principal reserve currency.

In this context it is obvious how significant a sacrifice of national sovereignty is inherent in monetary integration. The far-away aim is a European central bank; the nearer aims are a true monetary union and perhaps a partial pooling of reserves. All that we can conclude at this point in history, as we approach the end of the 1960's, is that European financial integration is a long way off and that the lack of it will be damaging to the Common Market economy throughout the coming decade.

HENRY SIMON BLOCH
WILLIAM BRUCE BASSETT

PREFACE

A DEFINITION OF FINANCE AND
THE SCOPE OF THE INQUIRY

THIS STUDY is limited to the financial aspects of European integration. The problems discussed have not been prominent, but they are rapidly becoming topical now that the complete realization of the Rome Treaty is in sight on all commercial matters.

"Financial" is a term that can describe many different things. In this book it is taken to mean anything happening in the circuit linking the act of saving by someone to the act of investing, or dissaving, by someone else. In terms of national accounts, this definition includes both the saving and investment account of a country or region, with the exception of self-financing by enterprises or by house owners, and the capital side of the balance of payments of a country or region.

National accounts do not provide a complete description because financial flows occurring within one sector are usually not shown and there is no presentation of creditor and debtor positions of enterprises, governments, regions, or countries.

Within a country, financial flows and balance sheets are affected by the institutional setup as well as by the government's use of the instruments of economic policy (mainly those of public finance and of credit). The main purpose of this study is to discover how European integration has modified this situation and to what extent financial flows or positions are influenced by the fact that the creditor and the debtor reside in different Common Market countries.

To achieve brevity, I have avoided many issues that are closely connected with my main subject. Among these are the following: all developments in European countries other than the six members of the Common Market (in financial matters, this means particularly Great Britain and Switzerland); all financial problems arising on a world-wide basis, such as the search for more international liquidity, the related dollar problem and access to European savings by capital-hungry American enterprises; and all matters affecting the underdeveloped countries, including Greece and Turkey, as well as the former African colonies which have special relationships with the European Economic Community.

FORMAT OF THE STUDY

Chapter 1 presents a brief history of all the nonfinancial aspects of European integration. These experiences in other areas must be recognized to appraise properly the present posture and possibilities of financial integration.

After the stage has been set in Chapter 1, the three approaches to European financial integration contemplated in the Rome Treaty establishing the Common Market (and occasionally in the earlier Paris Treaty setting up the European Coal and Steel Community) are described in turn. Chapter 2, of special interest to general economists, is devoted to harmonization of national economic policies. Chapter 3 examines a subject of particular interest to financial specialists in capital and money markets: the liberalization of capital flows. The international law approach to financial integration is presented in Chapter 4, where the possible creation of new European institutions is surveyed.

In Chapters 2, 3, and 4 a common pattern is repeated: first, the relevant clauses of the Rome Treaty, as interpreted in the light of treaty history; then, the results achieved by July 1968, that is, after nearly twelve years of the European Economic Community; and last, new developments that may be expected out of the main proposals made by various bodies or individuals for further progress in European integration, omitting those that do not have a chance of being implemented by 1970, the date originally fixed for the end of the transitional period of the Common Market.

PRELIMINARY CAVEATS

An economist who normally works in the area of macroeconomic or even nonfinancial microeconomic problems is struck by many dissimilarities when he approaches national and international financial matters. The most apparent are described below; these are caveats that must be considered by the reader throughout the book.

Financial statistics give the illusion of accuracy but are, in fact, very scanty; one is often left with a mixed collection of flows and stocks, and very little of the tidiness usual in national accounting or input-output analysis.

Capital is extremely fluid. It is not stopped by customs barriers or other physical obstacles. Avoiding exchange controls is quite easy for private persons and is not impossible for enterprises, particularly those of a financial nature. Hence, to a large extent, private capital movements occur in any case, short of very severe penalties (which are not exacted in Common Market countries for evasion of financial controls).

Whereas an external common tariff coincides with the Common Market, there is no such geographical frontier applying to capital flows. The "coordination of exchange policies of Member States in respect of the movement of capital between those States and third countries" intended in Article 70 of the Rome Treaty is still very much in its infancy. In fact, the main topics of exchange policies are discussed chiefly in groupings other than the Common Market—for example, the so-called group of Ten, in which the

United States, the United Kingdom, Japan, Canada, Sweden, and Switzerland which is in fact the eleventh member) are represented. Capital movements do not obey uniform rules at the frontier of the Six; instead, they are influenced by other nations' regulations, such as those that impede movements inward in the case of Switzerland, or outward from the United States or the United Kingdom.

Financial authors are often very conservative. Anything that smacks of money or credit is circumscribed by taboos; orthodoxy is praised nearly everywhere; pronouncements by central banks have mystical connotations; respectability and stability are more emphasized than innovation and expansion.

ACKNOWLEDGMENTS

I should like to express my appreciation to the following: Henry Simon Bloch, Adjunct Professor, Columbia University, who was the originator of the entire project, and Professor William Bruce Bassett of the Graduate School of Business who undertook the heavy responsibility of editorial work and revision in collaboration with Professor Bloch; the School of International Affairs of Columbia University, which financed the study and gave me a chance to improve it after discussions with the teaching staff and students; Jacques De Gruyse and Margaretha Lisein-Norman, who made very valuable contributions to the research work; Pierre Andre, R. Denuce, Max Frank, Herbert Glejser, Marcel Goblet, Lucien Morissens, Jacqueline Poelmans, and Claudio Segre, whose comments on early drafts resulted in many improvements; Judith Lourie, who assisted on certain linguistic problems.

E. S. KIRSCHEN

CONTENTS

*Financial Integration
in Western Europe*

1

A BRIEF HISTORY
OF EUROPEAN
INTEGRATION

A: EFFORTS BEFORE THE ROME TREATY[1]

Early Attempts

The desire for the creation of a united European power is not new. As early as 1305, Pierre Dubois, a lawyer from Normandy, called for a European state. Throughout the centuries that followed, Dubois had many followers, among whom should be mentioned Coudenhove-Kalergi and Briand. And, of course, a number of rulers tried to create a unified Europe and nearly succeeded.

What is new, however, is an attempt at integration by mutual agreement, with the support of large numbers of citizens and organizations. So far, this has happened only in Western Europe, although efforts at closer international cooperation are being made in other regions, especially Eastern Europe and Latin America.

As a result of this movement toward European integration by mutual agreement, new supranational institutions have been endowed with the power to use instruments enabling them to have their own international economic policy. This is the case in the

[1] For elaboration, see E. S. Kirschen and Associates, *Economic Policy in Our Time* (Amsterdam, North Holland Publishing Co., 1964).

European Coal and Steel Community (ECSC) and in the European Economic Community (EEC).

The First Success: the European
Coal and Steel Community

The ECSC was launched in May 1950 by Robert Schuman, the Foreign Minister of France, with the help of Jean Monnet. Schuman, who was born in Luxembourg and had served as an officer in the German Army during World War I, proposed the abolition of all obstacles to trade in coal and steel, not only for economic reasons but also as a gesture of reconciliation between France and Germany, and in particular between the heavy industries in the Creusot and the Ruhr (whose rivalry was considered by many people to have been one of the main causes of the war).

The treaty creating the ECSC—a first step toward economic and political integration in Europe—was signed in Paris in April 1951. It was eventually accepted by the Parliaments of France and West Germany and also by Italy and the Benelux countries (Belgium, the Netherlands, and Luxembourg), despite the opposition of the coal industry everywhere (whether nationalized or not) and of the steel industry in France. Other European governments did not join the ECSC because at the time they did not feel the political need. Some also believed that international cooperation should take place in the wider setting of the Organization for European Economic Cooperation (OEEC), even if this meant progress at a slower pace. Thus the Six came into being.

The First Setback: the European Defense
and Political Communities

Meanwhile, the need for the defense of Western Europe, which had led to the creation of NATO in 1949, again came to the foreground after the beginning of the Korean War. Two improvements in NATO appeared necessary: the rationalization of European armaments and the participation of West Germany. The rest of

Europe feared German rearmament without effective external control. West Germany, however, was opposed to rearmament unilaterally limited and controlled by the NATO countries; on the other hand, the United States and the United Kingdom did not wish to sacrifice any freedom of action in a more rigid organization. For these reasons, and also because of the early success of the ECSC in economic integration, the governments of the Six decided to create a specialized international authority: the European Defense Community (EDC). With NATO's approval, the treaty was signed in May 1952, subject to the approval of the parliaments of the signatory countries.

As envisioned by the draft treaty, the EDC comprised four institutions: the Commissariat, the Council of Ministers, the Common Assembly, and the Court of Justice, the last two belonging to both the EDC and the ECSC. A series of economic provisions dealt with common programs for the armament, equipment, supply, and infrastructure of the anticipated new European Defense Forces.

The treaty was ratified by the parliaments of five of the countries, but was rejected in 1954 by the French Chamber of Deputies, where it was opposed by a motley coalition of Communists and representatives of most other parties. This was the most important breakdown on the road to integration.

The abandonment of the project for a European Defense Community sealed the fate of a more ambitious plan for a European Political Community. The EDC draft treaty was not solely for garrison purposes; it contained an article on the convening of an assembly in charge of the preparation of a European federal constitution. Expecting ratification of the EDC treaty, the Consultative Assembly of the Council of Europe, in conjunction with the Assembly of the ECSC, gave an indication of what was being planned by proposing the creation of a bicameral European Parliament (one chamber elected directly, and one by the national parliaments), a European Executive Committee, and a Council of

National Ministers. These institutions were meant, among other purposes, to develop a common market in the aborted European Political Community.

The Rebound: the European Economic Community

After these failures, the governments of the Six returned to the international trade approach in their efforts to find another way to further European integration. The first promoters of this tactic were Paul-Henri Spaak and Jan Beyen, the Foreign Ministers of Belgium and the Netherlands, respectively, who were inspired by Jean Monnet, the main architect of the ECSC. During an ECSC conference at Messina in June 1955, the Benelux representatives suggested a new four-pronged approach:

1. A European Common Market for all goods and services.
2. A community for all types of conventional energy, thus adding gas, electricity, and oil to the coal industry already subject to the ECSC.
3. An inland transport community, covering rails, inland waterways, and roads.
4. An atomic energy community.

The second and third proposals were quickly abandoned under pressure of the industries concerned. The atomic energy project, however, survived. To some extent, this community was accepted because it gave the other countries a chance to control the German nuclear industry; but success was mainly due to a combination of sufficient enthusiasm and weak resistance: atomic energy was then very fashionable (it was considered in some circles to be the solution to an impending energy shortage in Europe) and the vested interests in this new industry were few and weak. To date, the Euratom Community, as it was finally called, has played a minor role.

Most important for European economic affairs was the eventual success of the first Messina proposal. After prolonged Common

Market negotiations, the European Economic Community emerged in March 1957, with the signing of the Treaty of Rome. Despite its economic emphasis, however, the EEC, as revealed by the history of the treaty, is closely, unavoidably, linked to political aims. This is the main reason why the Six were not immediately joined by other members of the OEEC. Specifically, the United Kingdom desired to keep its sovereignty and the Commonwealth preference system. Sweden, Switzerland, and Austria wanted to lead, rather than accept the bargaining disadvantages of adhering to a plan already in the process of formulation. The less developed countries of the OEEC—Portugal, Greece, Turkey, Ireland, and Iceland—feared a too-lively competition. In addition, most government administrators, particularly in Great Britain, did not believe that the Common Market would succeed and consequently did not attempt to persuade their governments to join.

B: OVERALL PHILOSOPHY OF THE ROME TREATY

After the decision had been reached in principle at Messina in June 1955, a group of experts was asked to produce a report on what was expected of the Common Market and other European institutions to be created. The report, written in 1956, is known as the Spaak Report.[2]

Since there appears to be no complete English translation publicly available,[3] we shall quote extensively from our own translation of this mimeographed document, wherever it is germane to this study, and thus make an important body of thought available to our readers. It should be understood that the authors of the

[2] Secretariat of the Intergovernmental Committee Created by the Messina Conference, *Report from the Delegation Heads to the Ministers of Foreign Affairs*, 120 F/56 (mimeographed document, Brussels, 1956).

[3] In June 1956, the Information Service of the High Authority of the ECSC published an unofficial translation in English of the main technical portions of the report on the Common Market prepared by the Intergovernmental Committee on European Integration (the Spaak Report), none of which is included in this book.

Report were not principally economic specialists and that their terminology does not always correspond to that used in the following chapters of this book. The subtitles are ours, and the order of items in the Report has occasionally been altered.

"The fusion of separate markets is a vital necessity. By increasing division of economic activity, it will eliminate the wasting of resources, and by greater security of supplies it will allow for the cessation of manufactures hitherto carried out regardless of cost. In an expanding economy, this division of economic activity consists not so much in a shift of existing manufactures as in increasingly rapid development of the most economic manufactures, in the common interest. Among competing producers the advantage will be determined less and less by national conditions. In the common market, success will again come to depend on the quality of men and management: pooling of resources leads to equal opportunities.

"This fusion of markets will lead to the large-scale introduction of modern manufacturing techniques. Even now some manufacturing techniques require such vast resources or machinery with such enormous yields as to exceed the scope of isolated national markets. Above all, in many sectors of industry the national market provides an ideal scale only for those companies which enjoy a practical monopoly. The advantage of large markets is that they combine mass production with the absence of monopolies.

"Furthermore, protectionist measures which eliminate foreign competition have particularly harmful repercussions upon the growth of production and upon the improvement in the standard of living, because they act as an incentive to eliminate internal competition. In a wider market, it is impossible to maintain outmoded methods which are a cause both of high prices and low wages; instead of remaining static, enterprises are subject to permanent pressure to invest: in order to develop production, safeguard their position, they must keep moving ahead."

The outgrowth of this philosophy in the Spaak Report is Article 2 of the Treaty of Rome:

It shall be the task of the Community, by establishing a Common Market and progressively approximating the economic policies of Member States, to promote throughout the Community a harmonious development of economic activities, a continuous and balanced expansion, an increased stability, an accelerated raising of the standard of living and closer relations between its Member States.

"These advantages of a common market can, however, only be achieved if time lags are allowed and if means are worked out collectively to permit the necessary adjustments, if an end is put to practices which distort competition among producers, and if cooperation is achieved between States to ensure monetary stability, economic expansion, and social progress.

"This is the fundamental reason why, desirable though the liberalization of trade on a world scale may seem in theory, a real common market will ultimately be feasible only among a limited group of States, although it may be hoped that this group will be as large as possible.

"In the first place, the complete elimination of customs tariffs between all States is inconceivable, while mere reductions in tariffs leave in existence inequalities which would distort the rational development of the various branches of industry. Moreover, the effects of State intervention to promote production are so extensive, the disparity between different sets of legislation can so deeply affect the relationship among industries, differences in the monetary evolution or in the pace of various countries' economic activity can so abruptly transform the price relationship or the flow of trade, that a common market is inconceivable without common rules, joint action, and, ultimately, a network of institutions to ensure its proper functioning.

"Although a common market can only be regional in character, that is, consist of States which feel sufficiently close to each other to introduce the necessary adjustments in their legislation and to base their policies on the need for mutual solidarity, this does not mean that such a common market is hostile to the rest of the world or that it dislocates the international division of labor. On the contrary, it lends the united economies the strength necessary to reduce protectionism throughout the whole area, to contribute to the general lowering of customs barriers throughout the world, and to establish with nonmember States closer relations than those they had previously maintained with each individual Member State."

Article 110 of the Treaty of Rome embodies this philosophy:

By establishing a customs union between themselves Member States aim to contribute, in the common interest, to the harmonious development of world trade, the progressive abolition of restrictions on international trade and the lowering of customs barriers.

The common commercial policy shall take into account the favorable effect which the abolition of customs duties as between Member States may have on the increase of the competitive strength of undertakings in those States.

The First Approach: Removing
All Obstacles to International Trade
between Common Market Countries

"The creation of normal competitive conditions and the harmonious overall development of the economies concerned hold out the hope that, by successive stages, it will be possible to *abolish all protectionist measures which at present impede trade and split up the European economy*; obstacles to trade not only consist of tariffs, quotas, or import monopolies, but also include restrictions in the apportionment of currency, discrimination in transport rates according to the country of origin or the destination of goods carried, as well as internal regulations, especially those governing services or agriculture, which in practice eliminate or restrict foreign competition.

"It is useless to eliminate protectionism in one place if it re-emerges in a different guise; thus, for instance, it would be difficult to hail as a step forward the replacement of generous global quotas by high tariffs. Measures must be applied logically all along the line.

"All this does not necessarily mean that the common market must in every case mean an entirely free market. Insofar as the

public interest (e.g., as regards services) or the nature of manufactures and markets (e.g., as regards certain agricultural products)
calls for regulations or organization, the common market itself
will require the gradual establishment of common regulations or
organizations.

"In modern economic conditions, the extension of markets and
competition is not in itself enough to bring about the most rational
distribution of economic activities and the most favorable pace of
expansion.

"The first factor to be taken into account is the scale already
attained by enterprise, or the existence of agreements among
enterprises, resulting in monopoly practices and opportunities
for discrimination and for market sharing. *Sound competition*
among enterprises is therefore necessary to ensure that dual pricing
does not produce the same effect as tariffs, that dumping does not
endanger economically sound manufactures, and that market
sharing does not take the place of market partitioning.

"The second factor consists of *extensive State intervention on
behalf of national industries.* Care should therefore be taken to
distinguish between aid calculated to promote the general interest
and develop production, and aid which is aimed at distorting the
competitive structure.

"In addition to actions which are deliberately calculated to
promote or protect national manufactures, *the incidence of the
disparity between legislation* or regulations governing competition
should also be carefully gauged."

The views expressed in these passages from the Spaak Report
resulted in the very important Article 3 of the Treaty of Rome:

For the purposes set out in Article 2, the activities of the Community
shall include, under the conditions and in accordance with the timetable envisaged in this Treaty:
(a) the elimination, as between Member States, of customs duties and
    of quantitative restrictions in regard to the import and export of
    goods, as well as of all other measures having equivalent effect;
(b) the establishment of a common customs tariff and of a common
    commercial policy towards third countries;

(c) the abolition, as between Member States, of obstacles to the free movement of persons, services and capital;
(d) the inauguration of a common policy in the field of agriculture;
(e) the inauguration of a common policy in the field of transport;
(f) the establishment of a system ensuring that competition in the Common Market is not distorted;
(g) the adoption of procedures permitting the co-ordination of the economic policies of Member States and the correction of instability in their balances of payments;
(h) the approximation of their respective national laws to the extent required for the Common Market to function in an orderly manner.

The abolition of obstacles to the free movement of capital, mentioned in Article 3(c), will be investigated in Chapter 3 of this study.

The Second Approach: the Creation of
New Common Institutions

"In addition to the pooling of existing resources, the common market fosters *the creation of new resources* by developing backward areas and utilizing unused labor forces; where necessary it contributes to the *productive reorientation of enterprises and workers*; and lastly, as a result of these measures, it fosters *the free movement of the actual production factors themselves, of capital and manpower*.

"As a first condition to common expansion, the labor force must be helped to achieve the necessary switch in employment, for there can be no progress without change. Hence, the importance of the retraining and resettlement measures, which protect labor against the dangers and expenses inherent in this progress.

"As a second condition, enterprises must be helped to redirect their manufactures, hence the importance of the means provided for industrial reconversion.[4]

---

[4] These two conditions gave rise, in the Rome Treaty, to the European Social Fund.

It is important to recognize as a third condition that, when communication is suddenly established between unequally developed regions, this does not automatically enable the less developed areas to catch up. Only if there is a deliberate policy to equip them with the necessary infrastructure for their development will they benefit to the full from differences in the cost of manpower or from the high return on investments. Hence the importance of regional development schemes and of measures designed to create local employment, which alone will avoid further widening of the gaps between levels of production and standards of living in the different areas."[5]

The Third Approach: the Coordination (Harmonization)
of National Economic Policies

"The role of States in modern economic life is also demonstrated by the differences they can create in the level of economic activity or of prices. This essential fact shows up both the dangers and the opportunities inherent in the creation of a common market.

"These differences are the principal cause of disequilibrium among the nations' balances of payments, that is, separately, each of the States may hamper the economic expansion of the others. Such differences could abruptly alter the terms of competition in a common market. Everything possible must therefore be done to avoid such differences or to overcome the effects thereof.

"But this joint action which, as the common market develops, will gradually become more regular and spontaneous, constitutes one of the most far-reaching results to be expected of the entire project. To evaluate the influence of the balance of payments on the potential for expansion, it is enough to compare the autonomy enjoyed in this field by the United States, with its vast internal market, to that of Great Britain, even though the latter stands at the center of a vast monetary area. Thanks to the co-ordination

[5] Here are the thoughts leading to the operation of the European Investment Bank, discussed in Chapter 4.

of economic policies in a common market, balance-of-payments problems would cease to jeopardize the continuity of expansion."[6]

The Main Institutions of the
Common Market [see Appendix I(A)]

Article 4 of the Rome Treaty created four main bodies which, de Gaulle or his successors permitting, may become comparable to American governmental institutions.

1. *The Commission* is a prefiguration of the U.S. President and his Cabinet.[7]

2. *The Council,* at present the most powerful body, will (it is hoped) in time resemble the U.S. Senate.[8]

3. *The Assembly,* now a very weak body, is expected to become analogous to the U.S. House of Representatives.[9]

4. *The Court of Justice,* is, of course, comparable to the U.S. Supreme Court.[10]

A fifth body, *the European Monetary Committee,* is not one of the main institutions of the Common Market, nor does it resemble any important American counterpart. Nevertheless, since the emphasis of our study is on European financial integration, it should be noted that the Rome Treaty did establish this consultative body in Article 105(2):

In order to promote the coordination of the policies of Member States in monetary matters to the extent necessary to ensure the operation of the Common Market, a Monetary Committee with consultative status shall be established with the following tasks:

[6] Chapter 2 of this book discusses the harmonization approach.

[7] The role of the Commission appears in Articles 155, 156, 158, and 163 of the Rome Treaty. These are reproduced in Appendix I(A).

[8] The important functions of the Council are described in Articles 145, 147, 148, and 149, as set forth in Appendix I(A).

[9] The central provisions concerning the Assembly are found in Articles 137, 138, 141, 143, and 144, which appear in Appendix I(A).

[10] Articles 164, 169, 171, 182, and 187, quoted in Appendix I(A), contain the main provisions describing the Court of Justice.

- to keep under review the monetary and financial situation of Member States and of the Community and also the general payments system of Member States and to report regularly thereon to the Council and to the Commission;
- the drafting of comments at the request of the Council or of the Commission or on its own initiative, for submission to these institutions.

The Member States and the Commission shall each appoint two members of the Monetary Committee.

The Rome Treaty did not attempt to force an immediate European economic and political revolution. Article 8 gave the Six twelve years to achieve the ends proposed. The following are the most important points in the transition plan of Article 8:

1. The Common Market shall be gradually brought into existence during a transitional period of twelve years. This transitional period shall be divided into three stages of four years each; the length of each stage may be modified in accordance with the provisions set out below.
2. A group of measures, to be simultaneously initiated and carried through, shall be allotted to each of these stages.
3. Transition from the first to the second stage shall be conditional upon a finding that the objectives specifically laid down in this Treaty for the first stage have been essentially achieved, and that, subject to the exceptions and in accordance with the procedures provided for in this Treaty, all obligations have been met.
. . .
5. The second and third stages may not be extended or curtailed except in accordance with a decision of the Council acting unanimously on a proposal of the Commission.
6. Nothing in the preceding paragraphs shall cause the transitional period to last more than fifteen years after this Treaty comes into force.
7. Save for the exceptions or derogations provided for in this Treaty, the expiry of the transitional period shall constitute the final date for the entry into force of all the rules provided for and for the completion of all the measures involved in the establishment of the Common Market.

The EEC is now entering the third (and last) stage of the provisional period. Its achievements are described in the ninth report of the outgoing Commission[11] and were commented upon by Walter Hallstein, then its president, in a speech to the European Parliament on June 29, 1966.[12] It is useful to compare these two sources with the action program drafted by the same Commission almost four years earlier.[13] In discussing these achievements, we shall also peer a little into the future and assume that some decisions, already reached in precise form, will be executed in fact.

The Successes

THE FREE MOVEMENT OF NONAGRICULTURAL GOODS BETWEEN THE SIX [see Appendix I(B)]. Quantitative restrictions on imports and exports have virtually disappeared by now, as well as customs duties on exports. Import duties, which were, of course, the main obstacle to intra-European trade, were submitted to eight successive reductions of 10 percent each between January 1, 1959, and January 1, 1966, that is, an average rate of 11.5 percent per year; a further reduction of 5 percent took place on July 1, 1967, and the total abolition of customs duties (of which only 15 percent remained) was to occur on July 1, 1968. At that time, 2½ years before the deadline set in the Rome Treaty this particular dream of free trade almost came true. Complete success was marred by last-minute adoption of "provisional" import restrictions and export subsidies by France to safeguard its balance of payments from the economic dislocations feared as an aftermath of the two-week general strike.

[11] Commission, European Economic Community, *Ninth General Report on the Activities of the Community* (Brussels, June 1966).

[12] *Europe*, June 29, 1966.

[13] Commission, European Economic Community, *Memorandum on the Action Program for the Second Stage* (Brussels, October 1962).

THE FREE MOVEMENT OF AGRICULTURAL GOODS BETWEEN THE SIX [see Appendix I(C)]. Here also, quantitative restrictions on trade have generally disappeared and customs duties have been reduced. By January 1, 1966, these duties had been reduced 60 percent, and they totally disappeared, well ahead of the initial deadline, on July 1, 1968. For the economist, however, the rejoicing will be marred by the knowledge that the agricultural common market will be heavily rigged in favor of producers inefficient at the world level.

The agricultural policy—which will be almost entirely in the hands of the Commission—is bound to favor European producers at the expense of European consumers. There is, however, one good point in a policy guaranteeing high incomes for the producers through high prices: the common European prices have been forcefully negotiated between the Ministers of Finance and Agriculture, a fact which seems to preclude any future modification in the relative exchange rates of the Six. By this devious route, an important step has been taken toward financial integration. In regard to the disadvantages of high agricultural prices, one can only hope for a progressive reduction in comparison with other European prices as the numbers of agricultural producers dwindle and their political strength recedes.

COMMON TARIFF ON GOODS FROM THIRD COUNTRIES.[14] With the temporary exception of France, a common external tariff also came fully into force on July 1, 1968. This tariff, in principle, will be the arithmetic average of the previous tariffs of West Germany, France, Italy, and the Benelux countries (Belgium, the Netherlands, and Luxembourg had already unified their duties before the Common Market started). Future reductions of the Common Market tariff will be negotiated in the General Agreement on Tariffs and Trade (GATT), within a framework similar to that of the Kennedy Round.

We omit the problems of tariffs on goods coming from Greece,

[14] Articles 18–29 of the Rome Treaty pertain to the common tariff.

Turkey, and former African colonies and do not attempt to discuss the possibility other European countries (e.g., Great Britain, Austria, Denmark) will either join the Common Market or establish special relationships with it. Since the beginning of 1967, the four national tariffs have gone 60 percent of the way toward the future common tariff, or toward this tariff minus 20 percent (in the latter case, in order to facilitate the GATT negotiations).

THE MERGER OF THE TREATIES AND THE EXECUTIVES. At the beginning of 1965, the governments of the Six decided as follows:

1. The treaties establishing the ECSC (1953), the EEC (1957), and Euratom (1957) would be merged.

2. There would be only one Council.

3. There would be only one Commission, which would be reconstituted with fourteen members but would have only nine members at a date not later than 1970.

This Commission began merged operations in July 1967, with the following locations serving as provisional seats for the Community institutions: Brussels, for most of the Commission's services and most of the Council meetings; Luxembourg, for the remaining activities of the Commission and of the Council, for the financial institutions, and for the Court of Justice; and Strasbourg, for the European Parliament.

The Half-Successes

Application of the Rome Treaty's provisions concerning freedom of establishment and freedom to supply services [see Appendix I(D)] is very complicated. There are no major issues, but a large number of minor ones exist. On these questions, sixteen directives have been adopted by the Council, on the proposal of the Commission. According to Walter Hallstein, former president of the Commission, the main bottleneck to faster work is the shortage of qualified international civil servants. Priority has been given to industrial and commercial activities, at the expense of the liberal professions, public works contracts, and some other matters.

The free movement of workers [see Appendix I(E)] is of particular interest because the movement of workers and that of capital are very often associated by economists under the heading of movement of the factors of production. In fact, however, the problems are very different; as the economic situation in Europe has entailed a shortage of workers everywhere, events have outrun the lawgivers. Nevertheless, the Rome Treaty is useful in preventing a return to the former protectionist practices of the national labor ministries.

Another half-success, gained in the fight against restrictive agreements and dominant positions,[15] involves a problem very familiar to Americans. It is still rather new, however, to Europeans, who have not yet quite awakened to the dangers of cartels, trusts, monopolies, and other concerted practices.

To this date, more than 38,000 notifications of agreements, decisions, and concerted practices have been made to the Commission. They have come mostly from enterprises or groups of enterprises seeking to obtain a "negative clearance" under Article 85, paragraph 3, or otherwise, showing that they are beneficial on the whole. To some extent, however, these notifications have been given in the hope of submerging the Commission's administration under an immense load of paper. Only 1400 cases have been settled.

Initiation of procedure by the Commission has occurred in just over 600 cases. Priority is given

- to actions pending before courts in the member states,
- to the discovery and examination of restrictions of competition that have not been reported,
- to horizontal market-sharing and quota agreements between manufacturers in various member states.

Decisions by the Commission were reached in 8 cases, and 54 enterprises modified their practices in order to avoid an unfavorable verdict.

In one very important case involving the principle of sole repre-

[15] Articles 85–94 of the Rome Treaty deal with the maintenance of fair competition in the Common Market.

sentation of a producer in one country by an agent in another country, the Court of Justice handed down a decision in favor of the Commission's rulings.[16]

In this area of trade regulation, it is difficult to avoid the impression that the Commission, in spite of good beginnings, will for many years be involved in very heavy administrative tasks.

The Failures

The Rome Treaty also contains important articles concerning other sectors; but there progress has lagged.

A main weakness is the *transportation* sector, despite the fact that it had already been partly included in the ECSC Treaty and was mentioned as a promising subject for European integration at the Messina meeting. The reason for the slowness of integration in transport is mainly lack of interest in this field by first-class politicians; there are many immediate pit-falls, because of regional or industrial interests, and few chances of spectacular success. However, the obstacles are not insurmountable, and in the long run integration in transportation can be expected.

Another slow starter is *social policy*, for example, equalization of wages for male and female labor, harmonization of social security, and training of skilled workers. Here the obstacles are due to weak drafting in the Rome Treaty and to the fear of jeopardizing agreements arrived at painfully on a national level between employers and labor unions.

Progress has also been virtually nonexistent in the field of *energy policy*. This is due, to some extent, to the fact that coal comes under the ECSC Treaty (which does not provide for a common external tariff or common external control of imports), and atomic energy is partly covered by the Euratom Treaty, leaving only electricity, gas, and oil to the care of Rome Treaty bodies. Although

---

[16] The decision of the Court of Justice, rendered in July 1966, declared an agreement of sole representation between a German manufacturer, Grundig, and a French importer, Consten, to be in violation of the Rome Treaty.

gas and electricity are nationalized in France and Italy, the state organizations responsible for them are very independent. Lastly, oil companies conduct their operations at a world level and have a strong Dutch financial basis. The Dutch Government as well as the oil companies also play a unique role in the extraction and distribution of the large national gas reserves found in Holland.

A common energy policy will come about only after the merger of the treaties, and will then have to tackle the very complicated problems of closing down most of the coal industry, organizing European networks for gas and electricity, separating peaceful and nonpeaceful uses of the atom, and taking on the oil interests. Obviously much time will be required to cope with all these matters.

2

HARMONIZATION

OF ECONOMIC

POLICY

A: A DEFINITION OF ECONOMIC POLICY[1]

ECONOMIC POLICY is "the deliberate intervention of governments in economic affairs in order to further their aims . . . such as preserving law and order, guarding the freedom of expression and choice, reducing social tensions, defending the country from outside attack, raising the population's standard of living, and making adequate provision for health and education."[2]

B: OBJECTIVES

Whereas aims belong to political philosophy and cannot be put into figures, objectives represent the translation of these aims into economic terms capable of measurement. There is no completely logical classification of objectives. Table 1 lists the most important

[1] Since the end of World War II European economic policy thinking has been dominated by Tinbergen. See J. Tinbergen, *On the Theory of Economic Policy* (Amsterdam, 1952) and *Economic Policy Principles and Design* (Amsterdam, 1956). We slightly modify the Tinbergen terminology in this study.

[2] See E. S. Kirschen and Associates, *Economic Policy in Our Time* (Amsterdam, North Holland Publishing Co., 1964), pp. 3–17.

TABLE 1
Present Main Objectives of
Common Market Countries

Name	Unit of Measurement (examples)	Acceptable Figures
SHORT-TERM OBJECTIVES		
1. Full employment	Ratio of unemployed to total labor force	2–3% (max.)
2. Price stability	Rate of increase of retail price index	1–2% per year (max.)
3. Adequate exchange reserves	Number of months of imports covered by reserves	3–4 (min.)
LONG-TERM OBJECTIVES		
4. Expansion	Rate of increase of the GNP at constant prices	4–5% (min.)
5. Promotion of internal competition	Share of market held by a single enterprise	30% (max.)
6. Promotion of international division of labor	Average rate of external tariff of the EEC	5–10% (max.)
7. Collective needs: (a) Defense	Ratio of government expenditures for the particular need	3–6% (max. & min.)
(b) Education, culture, and science	to the GNP	4–5% (max. & min.)
(c) Health		3–4% (max. & min.)
8. Improvement in distribution of income	Ratio of income of pensioned couple of manual workers to average family income	20–30% (min.)
9. Protection of particular: (a) branches of activity	Ratio of income per head in branch or region to per capita income in the	50–75% (min.)
(b) regions	whole country	60–75% (min.)

objectives of the Common Market countries and shows figures which seem to be acceptable to the present governments of the Six.[3]

In the context of the Rome Treaty and European integration, objectives should be categorized according to the extent to which their fulfillment is a Community responsibility or a national responsibility.[4] The following objectives are intimately linked to the Common Market:

1. Elimination of obstacles to the movement between the Common Market countries of goods, services, people, and capital.[5]
2. Improvement in the degree of competition between private enterprises.[6]
3. Organization of production in some branches of activity that are not left to the forces of the market, such as coal mining (which comes under the ECSC Treaty) or agriculture.[7]
4. The degree of protection for branches of activity subject to competition, such as steel or textiles.[8]
5. The security of supply of essential raw materials lacking in Europe, such as oil or iron ore.[9]
6. Aid to certain underdeveloped countries.[10]

None of these objectives is particularly important in the financial field, except for the elimination of obstacles to the movement of

[3] For further elaboration on the definition of the objectives, see E. S. Kirschen and L. Morissens, "Les motivations de l'homme politique en matière économique," *Cahiers économiques de Bruxelles*, No. 20, 1963, pp. 466–74.

[4] See Groupe d'Etudes de la Politique économique dans l'intégration Européenne, "Le transfert des objectifs économiques des autorités nationales aux autorités communautaries," *Cahiers économiques de Bruxelles*, No. 26, 1965, pp. 163 et seq.

[5] Articles 3(c), 12–17, 30–37, 48–73 of the Rome Treaty.

[6] Articles 3(f), 85–89 of the Rome Treaty.

[7] Articles 38–47 of the Rome Treaty.

[8] Articles 3(b), 18–29, 38–47, 110–116 of the Rome Treaty.

[9] Article 3(b) of the Rome Treaty and the ECSC Treaty.

[10] Articles 3(k) and 131–136 of the Rome Treaty.

capital, which will be fully discussed in the next chapter, and for aid to underdeveloped countries, which is not included in this study.

Although they are not intimately linked with its institutions, the harmonization of three short-term objectives is essential for the working of the Common Market: full employment, price stability, and adequate exchange reserves. The first two, and possibly the third, are dealt with in Articles 103–105 of the Rome Treaty. Article 104 states:

Each Member State shall pursue the economic policy necessary to ensure the equilibrium of its overall balance of payments and to maintain confidence in its currency, while ensuring a high level of employment and the stability of price levels.

Article 105, paragraph 1, calls for harmonization:

In order to facilitate the achievement of the objectives stated in Article 104, Member States shall coordinate their economic policies. They shall for this purpose introduce a policy of collaboration between their appropriate administrative departments and their central banks. The Commission shall submit to the Council recommendations on how to achieve such collaboration.

Collaboration must take the form of a harmonization of objectives. It is obvious that the common market in goods could not function properly if some governments tolerated a degree of unemployment or of inflation markedly different from that set as a limit by other governments. Similarly, uncoordinated surpluses or deficits in national balances of payments would create very grave problems. At this point, we are at the heart of the need for the harmonization of objectives.

The three short-term objectives must be viewed in the context of time. This necessarily leads us to consider the interrelated effects of national growth. In 1957, the year of the Rome Treaty, France and Italy were planning for something like 5 or 5½ percent per year, the Netherlands and Belgium were programing (a weaker word than planning, expressing wishful thinking rather than deliberate policy) for about 4 percent per year, and West Germany considered government intervention for growth as an invention of the devil. These wide differences of emphasis had to be taken into consideration. Consequently, Article 2 of the Rome Treaty, in mentioning the need for continuous and balanced growth, recognizes that this is a Community responsibility.

The following objectives are not mentioned in the Rome Treaty and can be committed, at least for a number of years, to the sole care of national governments:

1. Satisfaction of collective needs (education, research, health).
2. Improvement in the distribution of income.
3. Increase in the birth rate (religious factors are of significance in some countries).
4. Improvement in the structure of private consumption and savings, that is, more milk and housing, or less alcohol or loss of small savings.

C: HARMONIZATION OF OBJECTIVES IN PRACTICE

Full Employment

As shown in Table 2, unemployment has remained very low except in Italy, where the problem is largely long term and is being tackled through a general expansion policy.

Thus EEC policy in this area of responsibility has been limited to relatively small problems, such as the retaining and reinstallation of workers who are unemployed. However, there is little doubt that the Community would act vigorously if full employment were seriously threatened.

Price Stability

As shown in Table 3, price inflation is the real villain in Europe.

Between 1959 and 1962 the yearly price rises were kept within reasonable figures, but the process of inflation accelerated in 1963 and again in 1964. Italy and France were the first sufferers, followed by the Benelux countries. The fact that the rates of inflation were different in the various countries created a danger for the Community, as governments were tempted to resort to divergent remedies. As soon as the Commission realized the imminence of these disparate measures, it acted on public opinion and on the Council. In April 1964, the latter, acting under Article 103 of the

TABLE 2

European Unemployment Expressed as a Percentage of the Total Active Population(ᵃ)

	Germany		France	Italy	Belgium	Netherlands
	(ᵇ)	(ᶜ)				
1958	2.74		0.50	8.80	3.33	2.32
1959	1.91		0.75	8.52	3.78	1.82
1960	0.94		0.70	7.75	3.27	1.15
1961	0.63		0.60	7.08	2.53	0.82
1962	0.56	0.61	0.53	5.86	1.99	0.76
1963	0.68	0.73	0.51	5.39	1.65	0.77
1964		0.65	0.51	5.49	1.40	0.64
1965		0.57	0.73	5.97	1.67	0.74
1966		0.63	0.74	5.72	1.67	0.95

(ᵃ) National figures are not strictly comparable.
(ᵇ) Excluding Berlin.
(ᶜ) Including Berlin.

TABLE 3

Yearly Increases in the Prices of Consumer Goods (percent)

	Germany	France	Italy	Belgium	Netherlands
1958	2.1	15.1	2.8	1.0	1.7
1959	0.9	6.1	−0.5	1.8	0.8
1960	1.4	3.7	2.3	−0.1	2.5
1961	2.5	3.2	2.1	0.9	1.6
1962	3.4	4.8	4.7	1.5	3.3
1963	3.1	5.0	6.9	2.1	3.9
1964	2.4	3.4	6.0	4.5	4.9
1965	2.9	2.6	4.4	4.1	6.3
1966	3.4	3.0	2.3	4.3	5.6
1967	0.8	2.9	3.8	2.5	3.0

Rome Treaty, recommended to the governments of the Six that they give priority to price stability over all other objectives (including, in France, the well-honored objective of expansion) and act accordingly:[11]

(a) To maintain a liberal policy on imports;
(b) To limit the annual growth of public expenditure, if possible, to 5 percent;
(c) To finance any unavoidable spending above this ceiling by taxation, or from the marginal increases yielded by certain graduated taxes, or by increasing certain public charges;
(d) To finance any budget deficit persisting despite these measures by long-term borrowing;
(e) To maintain a restrictive credit policy and if necessary tighten it up;
(f) To explain to both management and labor the requirements and principles underlying the stabilization policy planned, with a view to an incomes policy for the rest of 1964 and for 1965 ensuring as far as possible that the increase of money income per head of the working population does not exceed the growth in real national product per head of the working population;
(g) To take special measures to curb demand in the building sector in those countries where demand exceeds supply, with the proviso that in countries where there is a shortage of school premises, hospitals, or low-cost dwellings, the construction of these should not be cut back or made more difficult;
(h) To consult, as may be necessary, with the other member countries on methods of financing any balance-of-payments deficit.

In 1965 these recommendations were altered to suit the divergent situations in the member countries. Among the changes, the necessity for not limiting investment over too long a period was stressed in several ways.

Exchange Reserves

Here the EEC was lucky during its first years. Exchange reserves, as shown in Table 4, were at comfortable levels and stayed

[11] Commission, European Economic Community, *Eighth General Report* (Brussels, 1965).

TABLE 4

European Exchange Reserves (expressed as a percentage of yearly imports)

	Germany		France		Italy		Belgium		Netherlands	
	(*a*)	(*b*)	(*a*)	(*b*)	(*a*)	(*b*)	(*a*)	(*b*)	(*a*)	(*b*)
1958	77		22		65		49		43	
1959	56		33		90		38		37	
1960	70		37		66		38		41	
1961	65		51		70		43		37	
1962	56		54		60		38		36	
1963	58	55	58	51	43	42	38	38	35	32
1964		48		51		51		38		30
1965		36		53		25.7		40		51.8
1966		37.5		48.4		43.1		27.2		25.4
1967		39.5		49.3		39.4		30.7		27.2

(*a*) Source: IMF, *Balance of Payments Yearbook.*
(*b*) Source: Statistical Office of the European Communities General Statistical Bulletin.

there. The only crisis occurred in Italy in 1964, when prices had got out of hand and speculation against the lira worsened the resultant balance-of-payments situation. But for the existence of the EEC, the Italian Government could have resorted to import restrictions in order to gain time for adjustment. In fact, it chose not to interfere with intracommunity trade (with some minor exceptions) and cured its economic illness by the rather painful method of inforced deflation; luckily, this was of rather short duration.

The Italian Government, however, did not seek financial help (in the form of short-term loans) from its partners' central banks, as provided for in Articles 108 and 109 of the Rome Treaty; it preferred to borrow from the United States, probably because it was quicker and easier to obtain a single large amount than a collection of smaller sums. As a consequence, the provision for mutual financial assistance was not tested on this occasion.

The coordination, among the Six, of international liquidity policies, mentioned in Article 70 of the Rome Treaty, is just beginning. According to the Monetary Committee,

The Council's decision of 8 May 1964 provided for consultations within the Committee on any decision or any important statement by Member States in the field of international monetary relations, in particular with regard to the general functioning of the international monetary system or where one or more Member States participate in major support operations aimed at helping nonmember countries. Consequently these topics were discussed in the Committee before they came up in the other bodies and institutions within which the Member States have been very active. In addition, the Committee has set up a working party whose task it is to confront and seek a common denominator for the points of view of the Member States so as to facilitate the work being done in the same field by these other bodies, notably by the Group of Ten. The Committee has also held discussions prior to the renewal of the EMA, to the increase in the IMF quotas and to the extension of the General Arrangements to Borrow.[12]

The difficulties in this collaboration stem from the well-known French views on the roles of gold and key currencies. No common policy of the Six has emerged so far. In fact, the controversy of the debates was escalated by the French Government in 1967 as it pushed more strongly for a study of the possibilities of increasing the value of gold.

Expansion

The formulation of a common expansion policy, although rather vague in the Rome Treaty itself, has been promoted by three factors:

1. The turning down of the French and Italian planned growth figures, as expressed in their national programs.
2. The weakening of the German opposition to any form of long-term government planning, programing, forecasting, or even projecting.

---

[12] European Economic Community, *Eighth Report on the Activities of the Monetary Committee* (Brussels, April 15, 1966), p. 1.

3. The lack of interest of the voters and of most politicians and civil servants in anything but immediate issues; in this matter, the psychological discount of time is very large.

In fact, since the beginning of the EEC, the growth rates of gross national product (GNP) have been quite respectable, as shown in Table 5.

TABLE 5

European Yearly Growth of GNP at Constant Prices
(in percent)

	Germany	France	Italy	Belgium	Netherlands
1958	3.2	2.6	4.4	−1.0	−0.1
1959	7.0	2.9	7.3	1.8	5.2
1960	8.9	7.4	6.7	4.5	8.9
1961	11.8	4.4	8.3	4.9	3.5
1962	4.2	7.0	6.3	4.9	2.6
1963	3.2	5.1	4.8	4.8	3.6
1964	6.5	5.3	2.7	6.7	7.6
1965	4.8	2.5	3.0	3.2	4.9
1966	2.3	4.9	5.9	2.8	2.8
1967	−0.1	4.3	6.2	3.5	5.0

Source: *La situation economique de la Communauté Européenne.*

The main issue regarding investment expansion policy among the Common Market countries turned out to be their differing attitudes toward private American investment in Europe. The French and, to a lesser extent, the German and Italian governments took a protectionist view and tried (sometimes unsuccessfully) to discourage new investment by European subsidiaries of American enterprises. They professed to be frightened at the idea of these enterprises reaping a large slice of the benefits arising out of the Common Market. The Benelux countries, on the other hand, welcomed American enterprises because they created up-to-date, high-productivity factories and helped to disseminate American techniques and know-how. These divergent policies were discussed in the Monetary Committee, which, evading the main issue, recently arrived at a conclusion linked somewhat to the American balance-of-payments difficulties:

Direct American investment has unquestionably contributed to economic growth in Europe, especially where accompanied by the transfer of advanced industrial techniques. But the flow of capital in all forms to the EEC has none the less become excessive, jeopardizing, at least for a time, the equilibrium of international payments and hampering the European countries in their fight against inflation. Consequently, the measures designed to curb exports of American capital to the Community certainly appear necessary if the objectives set forth above are to be achieved, though it is still too soon to say just what their impact on the European capital market will be.[13]

D: INSTRUMENTS

Instruments are economic policy variables upon which governments can act in order to reach the figures set for their objectives. Instruments of economic policy belong in five categories:[14]

1. Public finance, that is, government revenue and expenditure (except lending and borrowing).
2. Credit, including government lending and borrowing.
3. The exchange rate.
4. Direct controls, that is, government regulation of prices and quantities of goods and services traded.
5. Changes in the institutional framework. This last category of instruments is qualitative, whereas the first four are quantitative, subject to either discrete or continuous variations.

As far as European integration is concerned, this list can be supplemented by distinguishing the instruments according to degree of use by the community. Some instruments are totally or partly in the hands of community authorities. The most important of these are the following:

[13] *Ibid.*, p. 10.
[14] See Kirschen and Associates, *Economic Policy*, pp. 15–17, 148–149. Further work on the subject is in progress at the Institut d'Etudes Européennes of Brussels University.

Public finance: subsidies to enterprises, customs duties.

Direct controls: quantitative restrictions on private imports and exports, government imports, exchange controls.

Changes in the institutional setup: conditions of competition.

Some instruments are left to the national government, but their use has to be harmonized to some extent among the Six. This category comprises chiefly the following:

Public finance: indirect taxes on internal transactions and particularly on stock exchange transactions, direct taxes on business profits.

Credit: government loans and government guarantees to enterprises, central bank rediscount rate, control of borrowing by private enterprises, control of bank credit, control of credit by nonbanking institutions.

The exchange rate.

Direct controls: control of immigration, control of industrial operations, access to capital markets, access to stock exchanges.

Changes in the institutional setup: company laws.

Other instruments will probably remain in the sole care of national governments. Examples of this type are salaries of civil servants, direct taxes on household incomes, death duties, open market operations, control of installment buying, rent control, and changes in the extent of labor's influence on management.

As we have seen in Chapter 1, the authors of the Rome Treaty did not believe that European integration could be achieved through the play of market forces alone, and by setting up new institutions. With this in mind, they attempted to draft provisions for the harmonization of national policies. Unfortunately, the articles dealing with these provisions are generally very weak and the terminology is confusing; probably these defects are due, not to fuzzy thinking, but to the fact that the subject was new at the time of the negotiations and time was short.

We shall omit from this study some important problems (such as commercial policy and various subsidies or tax exemptions) in order to concentrate on the instruments of indirect taxes; the exchange rate; and the other instruments—generally unspecified in the Rome Treaty—that may be used by the Community to attain the important objectives of full employment, price stability, adequate exchange reserves, and economic expansion.

The harmonization of indirect taxes[15] was a problem that had to be tackled in the Rome Treaty because taxes of this type exert an important influence on the location of industry; widely differing national systems could very well nullify the integrative effects of the abolition of customs duties and other direct obstacles to international trade. Article 99 of the Rome Treaty reads:

The Commission shall consider how to further the interests of the Common Market by harmonizing the legislation of the various Member States concerning turnover taxes, excise duties, and other forms of indirect taxation, including compensatory measures in respect of trade between Member States. The Commission shall submit proposals to the Council; the latter shall decide upon the matter unanimously without prejudice to the provisions of Articles 100 and 101.

The problem would have been rather simple had it been enough to compute the average of national tax rates and to decide how the Six would gradually apply this average. However, apart from excises on alcoholic beverages, on tobacco, and on petroleum products, the national systems of taxation are very different. France, for instance, taxes the value added at each stage of industrial production (though not the value added in retailing), while Belgium taxes each sale by one enterprise to another (though not sales to private consumers). Moreover, the ratio of indirect taxes to total government income is high in France and Italy because indirect taxes are difficult to evade but is much lower in the Netherlands, where the progressiveness of direct taxes is appreciated as a means of reducing inequalities in income distribution.

[15] See Carl S. Shoup, *Fiscal Harmonization in Common Markets,* Vol. I: *Theory* (New York, Columbia University Press, 1967).

Thus, the Commission was left with a most difficult harmonization problem, both technically and politically.

The exchange rate, always an emotion-rousing instrument, is dealt with in Article 107 of the Rome Treaty:

1. Each Member State shall treat its policy with regard to rates of exchange as a matter of common interest.
2. If a Member State makes an alteration in its rate of exchange which is incompatible with the objectives laid down in Article 104 and which seriously distorts conditions of competition, the Commission may, after consulting the Monetary Committee, authorize other Member States to take for a strictly limited period the necessary measures, the conditions and details of which it shall determine, in order to meet the consequences of such alteration.

Articles 108 and 109 deal with balance-of-payments crises and refer to the granting of limited credits and other unspecified means of mutual assistance. However, co-ordination of the other two objectives, full employment and price stability, is nowhere explained in terms of instruments; the Treaty simply leaves this task to the Monetary Committee, composed of representatives of finance ministries and central banks (one of each per member country). These representatives are interested in price stability, but they are by no means the only ones to look after the economic policy instruments used for that objective: other official bodies in the national governments are responsible for such important instruments as the control of wages, agricultural prices, rents, transport rates, and, in some cases, restrictions on installment buying. The situation is still worse with respect to the objective of full employment: one shudders to think that responsibility for maintaining or regaining full employment, even in a depression period, as required by Article 104 of the Treaty, would be placed in the hands of the staunch financial orthodoxists on the Monetary Committee, without the help of administrative bodies that are controlling such instruments as public works or that are, at least, in closer contact with the suffering man on the street.

Contrary to the rest of the Rome Treaty, the economic policy section (Articles 103–116) definitely calls to mind pre-World War I orthodoxy, when only a few monetary and financial instruments were known, and even these were never used except in extreme circumstances.

E: HARMONIZATION OF INSTRUMENTS IN PRACTICE

Indirect Taxes[16]

As shown in Table 6, indirect taxes are a very important source of current government revenue in all Common Market countries. The individual figures fall into three groups: very high for France and Italy, high for Belgium and Luxembourg, and fairly high for Germany and the Netherlands.

Aside from revenue effects, any kind of alignment of indirect taxes among the Six is bound to entail major changes in a principal

TABLE 6

Share of Indirect Taxes in Government Revenue
in 1959

Country	Revenue Including Social Security Contributions (%)	Revenue Excluding Social Security Contributions (%)
France	48	68
Italy	43	59
Belgium	39	53
Luxembourg	33	47
Germany	31	44
Netherlands	31	41
United Kingdom	35	40
United States	34	39

Source: E. S. Kirschen and Associates, *Economic Policy*, p. 50.

[16] See Shoup, *Fiscal Harmonization*, Vol. II: *Practice*.

instrument of policy. For the policy maker, indirect taxes have two great advantages. First, they are politically convenient because their incidence is less obviously painful than that of income taxes. Second, they can be made highly selective. There is, however, a minor disadvantage in indirect taxation: if people expect a change in the tax, awkward economic effects may result. For example, if they believe the tax will rise, there may be a rush of anticipatory buying, producing such undesirable situations as an overaccumulation of inventories.

In trade-cycle policy, the usual practice has been to increase indirect taxes in the interest of price stability and the balance of payments (as in the Netherlands), and to reduce them in the interest of full employment (as in Italy). However, there is also the view that an increase in indirect taxes may worsen an inflationary situation by accentuating the wage-price spiral; as a consequence, some countries—Belgium regularly and France on occasions—have tried the reverse practice and have reduced indirect taxes as an anti-inflationary device. Refunds of indirect taxes or reductions in them for export industries have also been used in all EEC countries to improve the balance of payments.

Indirect taxes, in so far as they are levied on goods whose consumption increases rapidly as income rises, can also be regarded as built-in stabilizers. Taxes of this kind are usually regressive; proportionately, they fall more heavily on low incomes than on high incomes. However, in some instances luxury products are subject to very heavy taxes, which serve to improve income distribution. In some countries behind the high taxation on alcohol and tobacco there is the objective to improve the pattern of private consumption. In addition, tax reductions or differential rates are used to protect particular industries or regions, as, for instance, the textile industry in Belgium.

Usually, when there are general reductions in indirect taxes, other than for trade-cycle reasons, the objective is to encourage expansion, through either higher profits or lower prices. However, a general increase in indirect taxes, if coupled with a reduction in direct taxes on companies, could also be intended to aid expansion by encouraging investment at the expense of consumption.[17]

In June 1964 and in April 1965, the Commission proposed to the Council two directives for the establishment in all member countries, by January 1970, of a tax on value added (TVA), inspired by the French system. Finally, in February 1967, the Council adopted the TVA proposal.

The tax is to be levied on services and the sale of all goods, whether produced in one of the Six or imported into the Common Market. Taxes paid in any EEC country at the preceding stages of the economic circuit will be deductible.

The system is thus neutral as regards the place and methods of production and distribution. However, it is not neutral for some branches of activity that are now protected by specially low rates: agriculture, retailing, and one-man businesses.

All of the Six agreed on the principle of harmonization; the problem was one of method. France, Germany, and Luxembourg accepted the idea of a system based on a value-added tax, while the other three requested time for further studies. There were four main difficulties in reaching an agreement on the TVA.

1. Determination of the standard rate. Germany suggested 10 percent, but this was too low for France, Italy, and Belgium, which rely heavily on certain present indirect taxes that will have to be scrapped. On the other hand, rates of 13–15 percent, which gained acceptance in these countries, were opposed in the Netherlands and in Germany by representatives of the poor, who objected to the retrogressive features of indirect taxation. The solution for the latter countries, when the harmonization of rates becomes complete, might be to devote the extra resources resulting from the high rate of the TVA to bounties in favor of low-income households.

---

[17] See Kirschen and Associate, *Economic Policy*, pp. 54–56.

2. Determination of the beneficiaries of the special low rates. Can an advantage be granted to small shopkeepers, while the same advantage is denied to modern forms of retailing such as cooperatives or department stores?

3. Compensation for the victims of additional excise taxes.

4. The amount of protection the system entails for exports to third countries.

The Exchange Rate

In respect to the exchange rate, harmonization, although apparently vital, was not at first a success. According to the Monetary Committee:[18]

The revaluations of the German mark and the guilder decided on in March 1961 are due less to imbalances in relations with the other Member States than to imbalances in relations with nonmember countries. Although the Monetary Committee had studied this problem several times in the past, the final decisions on these changes were not preceded by perfect co-ordination within the Community.

The reason given by the Germans and the Dutch for not playing the game according to Article 107 of the Rome Treaty was the need for secrecy. This does not seem very convincing. In 1964, the procedure was tightened and the governments have agreed to consult with each other and with the Commission before making any change in their exchange rates. In any case, the decisions reached in matters of common agricultural prices reinforce powerfully the necessity for making the harmonization of exchange rate policies nearly compulsory. On May 30, 1968, the Council approved an obligatory set of rapid procedures to be followed for agreement on modifications in agricultural prices in the event of an alteration in existing exchange parities.

[18] European Economic Community, *Fourth Report on the Activities of the Monetary Committee* (Brussels, 1962), p. 9.

Credit

Each government tends to be proud of its instruments of economic policy and to believe that the experience of other governments is of little use to it. This attitude tends to disappear as the EEC produces reports assessing and comparing the effectiveness of instruments used by the Six.[19]

However, credit seems to constitute an exception. Instruments for regulating credit are simultaneously increasing in numbers and losing their efficiency. According to the Monetary Committee:[20]

Growing economic integration within the Community also means that the effectiveness of monetary measures taken at national level is declining. The more numerous forms of contact between member countries are enabling firms to avoid some of the effects aimed at when the authorities in their own country pursue a restrictive monetary policy. The difficulties the German authorities encountered in applying a restrictive credit policy in 1965 bear witness to this fact. In the past only the big companies were able to finance activities with money raised abroad, but now the growing interpenetration of commercial and banking relations in the EEC is making it possible for smaller firms to borrow abroad. This trend highlights the need for close international co-ordination if the effectiveness of credit policies applied is to be improved.

F: FUTURE PROGRESS IN THE USE OF INSTRUMENTS

Discussions on instruments among the Six are becoming more and more important as the national governments lose their sovereign control of exchange rates, exchange controls, customs duties, quantitative restrictions on trade, and control of immigration, and as their actions increasingly require new instruments or the improvement of old ones. Among the latter, public savings are bound to play an increasingly important role. At the same time, govern-

[19] European Economic Community, *The Instruments of Monetary Policy in the Countries of the European Economic Community* (Brussels, 1962).

[20] European Economic Community, *Eighth Report on the Activities of the Monetary Committee* (Brussels, 1966), p. 8.

ment transfers to households (through social security systems, public assistance, or otherwise) will not be allowed to continue their steady, uncoordinated increase, irrespective of the overall short-term economic situation.

Two important ideas have gained ground rapidly in the last few years, and it is hoped that they will be fully implemented by the end of 1970.

Of fundamental importance is the growing awareness of the necessity for considering economic policy as a whole. In the past, instruments of economic policy have often been entrusted to largely independent sets of officials. Generally, in all the Common Market countries, the central bank rate (for alleged secrecy) was manipulated with the prior knowledge of only the Governor, a few of his associates, and the Minister of Finance; the budget surplus or deficit (apparently for high political reasons) was fixed by the Minister of Finance and his collaborators; import quotas on goods competing with the production of protected industries were set by civil servants of the Ministry of Economic Affairs (for reasons not always considered very closely); and the immigration of workers or the rise in industrial wages was the responsibility of the Minister of Labor, who would normally consult industrialists and trade unions, but not his ministerial colleagues. This, of course, produced results similar to those that could be expected from an orchestra playing without a conductor. At present, coordination between policy makers in Common Market countries has improved markedly, with the exception, however, of the control of wages and other incomes.[21]

The second important idea gaining acceptance is the necessity for harmonizing instruments as well as objectives of economic policy among the Six.[22] The inflation of 1963 was a valuable lesson

[21] Commission, European Economic Community, *Ninth General Report on the Activities of the Community* (Brussels, June 1966), p. 144.

[22] On this point, see "Le transfert des objectifs économiques des autorités nationales aux autorités supranationales," *Cahiers économiques de Bruxelles*, No. 26, 1965.

for the Community as a whole because it showed the very large interdependence of economic illnesses among the Six and also of the attempted cures. The realization that there must be co-ordination on the Community level is, in a way, ironic when, as discussed above, coordination has hardly been reached on the national level.

According to Segre,[23] theoretically the most satisfactory solution of the coordination problem would be to entrust to the organs of the Community the definition and the carrying out of economic policy regarding short-term objectives. This would mean giving the Community (presumably by majority decisions) the right to prohibit and/or compensate for inappropriate uses of policy instruments by member states. A basic assumption, of course, is that governments would abandon, directly or indirectly, attributes of high political value. To ease this political pain, Segre favors a compromise, whereby the overall responsibility for anticyclical trade policy measures would be delegated to the Community after internal discussions, while the implementation of common policy through the instruments would be left to the individual governments, working within their own political, economic, and administrative frameworks.

The installation of this system could be a gradual process. Each time difficulties of unemployment, inflation, or balance-of-payments deficits arose, the necessity for coordination would become progressively more apparent, and as a consequence authority would gradually accrete to the system.

[23] C. Segre, "La coordination des politiques de conjoncture dans la CEE," Institut d'Etudes Européennes de l'Université de Bruxelles (1967).

3

THE
LIBERALIZATION
OF CAPITAL FLOWS

A KNOWLEDGE of the Spaak Report[1] is extremely helpful in properly interpreting the Rome Treaty, especially the provisions concerning capital movements. The remainder of the present section, therefore, is devoted to our translation of the Spaak Report's thoughts in this field.

"The free movement of capital is distinct from transfers connected with goods, services, or the movement of manpower, and includes the unrestricted right of nationals of Member States to acquire, transfer, and utilize within the boundaries of the Community, capital originating within the Community.

"By making more money available to finance investments and by allowing existing resources to be better deployed over a broader area, the freeing of capital movements leads to an improved use of the savings potential and a more rapid creation of the means of production. Normally speaking, capital movements should help to

---

[1] Secretariat of the Intergovernmental Committee Created by the Messina Conference, *Report from the Delegation Heads to the Ministers of Foreign Affairs*, 120 F/56 (mimeographed document, Brussels, 1956). See Chapter 1, part B. p. 5.

X

avoid disequilibrium between the balances of payments of different Member States and to harmonize the cost factor represented by rates of interest and other financial burdens.

"Controls on the movement of capital will always be illusory in part, for there is no proof that a nation has more capital at its disposal or makes more efficient use of it by preventing its own capital from leaving the country, since this also discourages the influx of fresh capital from abroad. But in order to overcome this prejudice, and to eliminate the barely disguised nationalism of many of the existing regulations, one must also appreciate that very real difficulties will have to be solved if the freeing of capital is to foster economic improvement instead of causing disequilibrium.

"The most obvious problem is that differences in monetary policy or doubts about the stability of currencies create *speculative movements of capital* which may take the form of a sudden exodus: in this way capital stops flowing toward areas which are in the greatest need of money, where rates of interest are higher or where there is a deficit in the balance of payments. The gradual development of the Common Market, the rules drawn up to regulate its functioning and the mechanisms to be established within its framework, would provide the best solution for these differences and would help to eliminate the resulting speculation.

"The second obstacle resides in the fact that capital may move from country to country, not for purposes of investment but to *escape abroad, in order to benefit from a less stringent application of exchange controls elsewhere.* The free movement of capital within the Common Market will therefore call for a mutually agreed attitude, which should of course be adjusted to prevailing economic circumstances and which, in the last stage, would result in equal freedom or in a uniform degree of control.

"A third obstacle resides in *differences between the laws of various countries, especially as regards taxation,* which fundamentally affect the comparative yields of investments. This is one particular aspect of the distortion which will need to be corrected and which, as regards direct taxation of profits at all events, can be avoided only by harmonizing both the taxable basis and the rate of taxation in the various Member States.

"The fourth danger is that, instead of aiming for the under-developed areas, *capital may move away from them toward more developed areas*: this means that the basic conditions would be lacking which are needed to ensure the profitable nature of invest-ments in less developed areas. It is fundamental aim of the In-vestment Fund (later known as the European Investment Bank) to solve this problem.

"We have thus shown that it will be possible to avoid the diffi-culties and dangers inherent in the free movement of capital by modifying certain basic economic factors. Yet, by its very nature, this is not a field easily subjected to rigid rules and automatic procedures. It is impossible to determine the various stages in advance. There is no valid basis for reference, and a timetable drawn up, say, in accordance with the nature of transfers might even jeopardize the success of the whole operation.

"On the one hand, the *basic conditions already mentioned should be brought about* and the resulting effects carefully observed in order to determine the feasible pace of liberalization accordingly.

"On the other hand, *priority should be given to certain types of transfer.*

"(i) *The transfer of interest on loans and of profits* or invest-ment revenues is already free to a great extent, but this liberaliza-tion should be consolidated in order to strengthen the confidence of investors.

"(ii) *Direct investments* are still in many cases subject to con-trol, either for protectionist motives or as a result of the currency position; controls of a protectionist nature should be abolished first of all, but the others too should disappear as soon as possible, since the free play of competition is hampered when an enterprise is virtually prohibited from transporting its installations or from establishing subsidiary installations on the territory of another State where the competitive structure is more favorable.

"(iii) Some degree of liberalization has already been achieved as regards *the transfer of securities and the subscription of bonds and shares*: this should be further consolidated and extended in order to achieve equality for direct investments and share subscriptions, and to facilitate the intercommunication of financial markets. Internal regulations governing the right and the means to float issues, which are designed to protect the monetary balance, could in theory remain dissimilar, providing discrimination were eliminated between issuing houses or subscribers so long as the parties involved are nationals of the Member States.

"During a transitional period of approximately ten years some *protective clauses* would be unavoidable, in order to prevent speculative movements of capital from affecting the balance of payments. But when the Common Market is fully established such clauses would doubtless be ineffectual since the free transfer of goods and services would greatly help to conceal any exodus of capital."

B: THE ROME TREATY[2]

The liberalization of capital movements is given seven Articles (67–73) of the Rome Treaty but remains, nevertheless, rather vague when compared with the prescriptions and timetable concerning the common market for goods. It appears that the authors of the Rome Treaty did not consider the liberalization of capital movements as something to be achieved for its own sake (for instance, the right of an individual to buy a house or securities in another country), but rather as a means of facilitating the free movement of goods and services.

The main provisions on capital flows are contained in Articles 67 and 68, which read as follows:

Article 67
1. During the transitional period, Member States shall, in so far as may be necessary to ensure the proper functioning of the Common

---

[2] For a comment on the treatment of capital movements by the Rome Treaty, see C. Segre, "Capital Movements in the European Economic Community," *Banca Nazionale del Lavoro Quarterly Review* (Rome), March 1962.

Market, progressively abolish between themselves restrictions on the movement of capital belonging to persons resident in Member States and any discrimination based on the nationality or on the place of residence of the parties or on the place where such capital is invested.

2. Current payments connected with movements of capital between Member States shall be free from all restrictions not later than the end of the first stage.

Article 68

1. Member States shall, as regards matters which are the subject of this Chapter, be as liberal as possible in the granting of such exchange authorizations as are still necessary after this Treaty comes into force.

2. Where a Member State subjects the movements of capital liberalized in accordance with the provisions of this Chapter to its domestic rules governing the capital market and the credit system, it shall do so in a nondiscriminatory manner.

3. Loans intended for the direct or indirect financing of a Member State or of its territorial subdivisions shall not be issued or placed in other Member States unless the States concerned have reached agreement on this. This provision shall not preclude the implementation of Article 33 of the Protocol on the Statute of the European Investment Bank.

It is evident from these provisions that the abolition of discrimination based on nationality is considered particularly important.

The procedure for liberalization of capital flows is set forth in the Rome Treaty. The Commission is given the right of initiative, through the preparation of directives that are presented to the Council after approval by the Monetary Committee. As detailed in Articles 69 and 70, the Council either approves or vetoes these proposals.

Article 69

The Council, on a proposal of the Commission which for this purpose shall consult the Monetary Committee provided for in Article 105, shall issue the necessary directives for the progressive implementation of the provisions of Article 67. It shall so act by a unanimous decision during the first two stages and subsequently by means of a qualified majority vote.

Article 70

1. The Commission shall propose to the Council measures for the progressive coordination of the exchange policies of Member States in respect of the movement of capital between those States and third countries. The Council shall by unanimous vote issue directives for this purpose. It shall endeavor to achieve the highest possible degree of liberalization.

2. Where the measures taken in accordance with the preceding paragraph do not permit the elimination of differences between the exchange rules of Member States and where such differences lead persons resident in one of the Member States to make use of the transfer facilities within the Community, as provided for under Article 67, in order to evade the rules of one of the Member States in regard to third countries, that State may, after consulting the other Member States and the Commission, take appropriate measures to overcome these difficulties.

   Should the Council establish that such measures are restricting the free movement of capital within the Community to a greater extent than is required for the purpose of the preceding paragraph, it may, acting by qualified majority vote on a proposal of the Commission, decide that the State concerned shall modify or abolish these measures.

As requested in the Spaak Report, the Rome Treaty limits protective measures to the period of transition. What happens, however, if new restrictions appear necessary because of strong disturbances in the capital market of a member state? Additional measures can be taken after approval by the Commission, which will consult the Monetary Committee; but if matters become really urgent, any member state can make the decisions it deems necessary and only thereafter will these be examined by the Commission in consultation with the Monetary Committee. This procedure was used by France in June 1968.

If misused, this national safeguard could turn into a serious impediment to the process of liberalization. Presumably, the Commission will try to avoid balance-of-payments difficulties being used, as in the past, to disguise protectionism in capital markets.

Savings and Investment Accounts

Savings and investment accounts are shown in Table 7 for all EEC countries except Luxembourg.[3] Total investment in 1964 was approximately 67 billion dollars, of which roughly 40 percent was covered by depreciation allowances, 20 percent by government savings, 8 percent by company savings, and 32 percent by household savings. Non-European savings, arriving in Europe through the deficit in the current balance-of-payments accounts of France and The Netherlands, were negligible.

From Table 7 it can be seen that, if depreciation, savings by companies, and the part of savings by households used for financing the purchase of private houses are subtracted from the total means of financing investment, something like 35 billion dollars is left. About all of this amount is invested through economic agents other than the savers themselves; it represents savings by government and households that account, respectively, for 15 and 20 billion dollars.

The Financial Markets

Most government savings find their origin in taxes and are used to finance government investment (in addition, of course, to government borrowing). Savings by households, to the extent of 20 billion dollars, were collected in 1964 on the financial markets by a number of intermediaries. The most important were the following: governments (for the financing of the excess of their investments over their savings), public enterprises, stock exchanges, banks, savings institutions, and other financial institutions, such as insurance companies and pension funds.

[3] According to OECD, *Standardized System of National Accounting* (Paris, 1958).

TABLE 7
The 1964 Capital Account of the EEC Countries
(billions of dollars)

	Germany	France	Italy	Netherlands	Belgium	Total
Investment						
Gross fixed capital formation (including home building)	27.49	18.45	10.45	4.23	3.10	63.72
Increase in stocks	1.18	1.48	0.24	0.53	0.07	3.50
Total investment	28.67	19.93	10.69	4.76	3.17	67.22
Financing of investment						
Depreciation	10.57	8.00	4.54	1.52	1.49	26.12
Government savings	7.69	3.99	1.74	0.70	0.21	14.33
Company savings	1.36	1.63 }	5.08 }	0.64	0.29 }	26.39
Household savings	9.32	5.18 }		1.69	1.20 }	
Excess of imports over exports (balance of current account)	−0.27	+1.12	−0.66	+0.20	−0.01	+0.38
Total means of financing investment	28.67	19.93	10.69	4.76	3.17	67.22
Ratio of total investment to GNP	28	23	22	28	21	25

Sources: *CEE L'Bulletin général de statistiques*, No. 1, 1965;
Banque Nationale de Belgique, Bulletin d'information et de documentation, March 1966.

Of course, the volume of the transactions on the financial markets is much higher than 20 billion dollars, for three reasons.

1. Several intermediaries can intervene between the saver and the ultimate investor.
2. Old debts are reimbursed and re-lent during the accounting year.
3. Non-European savers and investors have access to the European markets.[4]

As most of the investment is in fixed capital (increases in stocks or inventories account for only 10 percent of net investment), it is bound to take the form of construction or machines having a life of 10–30 years. As a consequence, one of the main roles of the financial intermediaries is to give savers the illusion that much more than 10 percent of their savings is used for short-term purposes; another is to collect small driblets of savings into streams large enough to suit the investors.[5]

Most of the important statistics on European capital markets are assembled in the annual reports of the European Investment Bank. This source was used for the 1964 figures in Tables 8 and 9. According to Table 8, about 10 billion dollars in new securities was issued in 1964, of which three quarters, that is, 7.5 billion dollars, went to enterprises. According to Table 9, enterprises also obtained some 11.5 billion dollars in medium- and long-term loans from intermediaries other than stock exchanges. The sum of these two figures is 19 billion dollars. Unfortunately, this picture of financial flows is far from complete because figures are available neither for short-term money obtained by enterprises from financial intermediaries, nor for small, direct, short-term borrowing from households.

[4] The best figures on European markets (although somewhat dated) can be found in *Economic Policy and Practices: a Description and Analysis of Certain European Capital Markets*, by U.S. Congress, Joint Economic Committee (Washington, 1964).

[5] In addition to this study and the European Investment Bank's annual reports, information on Germany, the Netherlands, and Belgium (and also Great Britain) is available in *Capital Markets in Europe*, by an economic research group of four European Banks (London, 1966).

Intra-European Capital Flows

So far we have referred to European capital markets, but of course we want to know to what extent we can speak of one European capital market comparable to the common market for industrial or agricultural goods. There is no reason, a priori, why savings originating in one country should go to financial intermediaries in the same country and from them to investors, still in the same country; obviously, this geographical pattern of savings and investment does not hold true for any one region within a country.

Table 10 shows the capital side of the balance of payments of EEC countries; Belgium and Luxembourg appear together, as they have formed a monetary union. There is no breakdown of the figures into intra-European and extra-European flows, but Table 11 gives nonofficial long-term capital flows inward and outward for four countries.

Intra-EEC flows in general are rather small, the only figure larger than 100 million dollars being for direct investments in Italy by residents of other EEC countries. The intra-EEC balances for the four countries listed in Table 11 are as follows:

Germany:	− 67 million dollars
France:	+ 79
Italy:	+239
Netherlands:	− 17

These figures are tiny when compared to total European private savings of 20 billion dollars; in fact, for each of the four countries, nonofficial intra-European capital flows are smaller than capital flows originating in the United States.

D: THE PRESENT STATE OF EUROPEAN CAPITAL MARKETS[6]

Gold can be freely bought and sold in all of the Six and can be imported and exported without restrictions in Belgium, Germany, Luxembourg, and, as of February 1967, in France. The French

---

[6] See *Pour améliorer le fonctionnement des marchés des capitaux.* L'observateur de l'OECD, Paris, Avril 1967; *The Development of a Euro-*

restrictions on the export of gold were temporarily reimposed on May 29, 1968, to stem a run on the franc occasioned by the national strike. This relative lack of controls provides a favorable setting for transactions. For example, daily trading in gold on the Paris stock exchange may reach a volume of 2 million dollars.[7]

The main stock exchanges of the Common Market countries are located in Paris, Amsterdam, Brussels, Luxembourg, Milan, Düsseldorf, and Frankfurt. The volume of trading on these exchanges is relatively small. This is illustrated by comparing their share (not bond) turnovers with that of the New York Stock Exchange. The ratios obtained are 0.55 percent for Brussels, 0.93 percent for Amsterdam, and 2.72 percent for Paris. The ratio for Luxembourg is very small, and the figures for Milan, Dusseldorf, and Frankfurt are not listed because their volumes are closely guarded secrets: neither of the German exchanges wants its percentage to be known lest it be smaller than that of its competitor. Comparison with the New York Stock Exchange is not needed to highlight the thin character of the stock markets in the Community; even more illuminating may be the fact that the turnover of shares in London is more than five times higher than in Paris.

Only a few European companies have their shares quoted on a European stock exchange outside their own country. Table 12 lists the cases where quotations are obtained on at least three stock exchanges, two of which are located outside the country where the company has its main activity. The list is not very long, as many savers prefer to buy shares of companies they know rather well, meaning, of course, companies in their own countries.

Table 13 lists the main American shares quoted on at least two European stock exchanges. American shares, for various reasons, are not often listed on European stock exchanges. This is particu-

pean Capital Market. Report of a group of experts appointed by the EEC Commission (the so-called Segre Report), dated November 1966, but published in May 1967, Brussels; and Ira D. Scott, "European Capital Markets," *National Banking Review,* December 1966, Washington.

[7] C. Bourillon, "La circulation des capitaux dans le Marché Commun," Le Crédit du Nord (Paris, 1963).

TABLE 8

Net Issues of Securities in EEC Countries in 1964
(billions of dollars)

	Germany	France	Italy	Netherlands	Belgium	Total[a]
Bonds						
Public sector	1.53[b]	0.17	0.37	0.13	0.34	2.53
Private sector	1.79	1.08	1.95	0.04	0.08	4.94
Total	3.32	1.25	2.32	0.17	0.42	7.47
Shares	0.58	1.01	0.89	0.06	0.22	2.75
Total issues	3.88	2.26	3.21	0.23	0.64	10.22

Source: Banque Européenne d'Investissement, *Rapport annuel*, 1965, pp. 35, 36.
[a] Excluding Luxembourg.
[b] Some of the money raised in Germany by the public sector is ultimately lent to the private sector.

TABLE 9

Medium- and Long-Term Credit Available to Private Enterprises in 1964
(billions of dollars)

	Germany	France	Italy	Netherlands	Belgium	Total[a]
Gross	6.82	3.63	2.72	1.33	0.65	15.15
Net, i.e., after deduction of resources already counted in Table 8	5.11	3.04	1.58	1.24	0.63	11.60

Source: Banque Européenne d'Investissement, *Rapport annuel*, 1965, pp. 33, 34.
[a] Excluding Luxembourg.

TABLE 10

The Capital Side of the Balance of Payments of the EEC in 1964[a]
(millions of dollars)

	Germany	France	Italy	Netherlands	Belgium-Luxembourg
Total balance of payments					
Gold	−404	−554	+ 237	− 86	− 78
Private capital, short term	+ 11	+212	−1221	+251	+214
Private capital, long term	+197	+527	+ 843	+137	−172
Official capital, short term	+176	−262	− 455	−160	−172
Official capital, long term	−493	− 81	− 85	− 34	+ 28
Total	−513	−158	− 681	+108	− 8
Intra-EEC balance of payments[b]					
Private capital, short term	−136	− 65	− 56	+102	+ 6[b]
Private capital, long term	0	+80	+225	− 1	
Official capital, short term	+ 7	0	− 2	− 1	+78
Official capital, long term	−137	− 2	+ 59	− 6	
Total	−266	+13	+226	+ 94	+84

Source: *CEE Bulletin général de statistiques*, No. 12, 1965.

[a] The data do not coincide entirely with those of Table 11.
[b] Including all transactions by commercial banks.

TABLE 11

Nonofficial Long-Term Capital Flows in 1964
(millions of dollars)

Origin	Germany	France	Italy	Netherlands
INWARD				
EEC	123	139	282	80
Direct	38	87	234	17
Portfolio	— 1	32	10	52
Others	86	20	38	11
United States	234	141	374	8
Direct	99	109	127	50
Portfolio	13	5	2	— 72
Others	122	27	245	30
From other countries	208	323	417	208
Direct	44	131	174	23
Portfolio	117	101	— 9	110
Others	48	91	242	75
Totals	565	603	1073	296
OUTWARD				
EEC	190	60	53	97
Direct	42	62	25	74
Portfolio	79	— 3	3	— 12
Others	69	1	25	35
United States	1	— 57	56	— 2
Direct	4	2	72	10
Portfolio	— 6	— 49	5	— 14
Others	3	— 10	— 21	2
To other countries	263	73	61	86
Direct	63	98	56	65
Portfolio	135	— 26	6	12
Others	65	1	— 1	9
Totals	454	76	170	181
Balance	+111	+527	+903	+115

Source: Banque Européenne d'Investissement, *Rapport annuel*, 1965, p. 46.

TABLE 12

Shares of European Companies Quoted in at Least Two Other European Countries[a]

Home Country	Company	Amsterdam	Brussels	Paris	Luxembourg	Frankfurt or Dusseldorf
Germany	AEG	x		x		
	Hoechst	x	x	x		
	Rheinische	x		x		
	Siemens & Halske	x	x			
Belgium	Cockerill-Ougree	x		x	x	
	Cofinundus	x		x		
	Gevaert	x		x	x	
	Wagon-Lits	x		x		
France	Banque de Paris et des Pays-Bas	x	x			x
	Pechiney	x	x			x
	Peugeot	x	x			
Italy	Montecatini	x	x	x		x
	Pirelli	x	x	x		x
	Snia Viscosa		x	x		x
Luxembourg	Arbed	x	x	x		
Netherlands	Philips Gloeilampen		x	x	x	x
	Robeco		x	x		x
	Royal Dutch		x	x	x	x
	Unilever		x	x	x	x

[a] No foreign shares are quoted in Milan.

TABLE 13

American Shares Quoted in at Least Two
European Stock Exchanges[a]

Company	Brussels	Paris	Amsterdam	Frankfurt or Dusseldorf
Aluminum Co. of America (Alcoa)	x			x
American Tel. & Tel.	x	x		x
Dow Chemical	x		x	
du Pont de Nemours	x	x	x	x
Eastman Kodak	x	x	x	x
Ford Motor	x	x	x	x
General Electric	x	x	x	x
General Motors	x	x	x	x
Goodyear Tire & Rubber	x	x	x	x
International Business Machines (IBM)	x	x	x	
International Tel. & Tel. (ITT)	x		x	x
Standard Oil Co. of New Jersey	x	x	x	x
U.S. Steel	x		x	x
Union Carbide Corp.	x		x	
Westinghouse Electric	x		x	
National Biscuit		x	x	
Kennecott Copper		x	x	x
Socony Mobil Oil		x	x	
Merck		x	x	
Monsanto Chemical		x	x	
Procter and Gamble		x	x	
Gillette Co.		x	x	
Philip Morris		x	x	

[a] No foreign shares are quoted in Milan.

larly true of European subsidiaries of American companies (e.g., General Motors or Ford) because the American firms often want to keep complete control, in spite of European demands for a part of the profits and a share in the management.

In these circumstances, some experts believe that U.S. corporations might benefit themselves and certainly their public image if they turned to more equity financing, giving Europeans a real stake in their foreign operations. The convertibles recently issued are a small start in this direction, but only that. For the financial affiliates doing the borrowing are, after all, 100 percent owned by the parent company.[8]

Bonds are the principal finance instrument for which there begins to be something like a European market. Of course, most of the issues are still put on the market of one country by a resident of that country and subscribed to by a saver in the same country. However, exceptions are becoming more and more numerous, partly through the influence of syndicates of bankers from several countries.[9]

Although the borrowers in the European sector of the international capital market are well known, the identity of those who buy their paper is something of a mystery. A large percentage of the money passes through Switzerland, where bankers, by tradition and by law, are committed to secrecy as to what their clients are doing. These clients include citizens of France, Belgium, and Germany as well as a substantial number of South American millionaires and Arabian oil sheiks. However, the use of Swiss banks as a conduit is becoming of lesser importance as recent Swiss administrative and fiscal policies have resulted in more stringent control of the flow of funds.[10]

---

[8] John Davenport, "The Fine Art of Raising Cash Abroad," *Fortune*, May 1966.

[9] H. J. Abs, *Le Marché Européen de valeurs et d'émissions* (Knokke, 1964).

[10] For a description of American borrowers, see E. Schwarzenbach and J. Zwick, "The European Response to U.S. Capital Restrictions," *National Banking Review*, March 1966.

A complex variety of devices is employed in Europe for controlling and screening capital outflows. These range from principal reliance on licensing to the application of indirect control by requiring capital payments to go through special exchange markets. These markets need not be supported by the central bank because, under the Articles of Agreement of the International Monetary Fund, the maintenance of par values within a percentage point is obligatory only for current, as opposed to capital, transactions. Since these exchange rates may vary considerably, depending upon government intervention policy, they can provide a market check on disproportionate capital flows between countries. At the same time, however, with the small capital markets of each member state, they serve as impediments to the development of a European capital market. Nevertheless, these capital exchange markets are specifically authorized by the EEC directives on the liberalization of capital flows.

If a potential lender's usual currency is not that of the bond issue (and sometimes even if it is), he will consider possible exchange losses through devaluation or revaluation before redemption or maturity of the issue. This added element of insecurity may be especially important to the class of investors purchasing bonds. However, between the Six, modifications in exchange rates are now very unlikely. The present degree of economic union practically necessitates fixed rates of exchange between member states.

More specifically, according to the Commission's action program issued for the second stage of Community evolution in October 1962, such a freezing of exchange rates is essential on four grounds. First, the elimination of all barriers to trade within the Six makes any "major modification" of rates extremely disruptive to established trade patterns. Second, since the agreement on common prices for grain and other basic agricultural products has been concluded, any exchange rate adjustments would cause sudden changes in domestic farm prices and in farm incomes. Third, fixed rates of exchange "firmly guaranteed by appropriate institutions and methods" are a precondition for the free flow of capital throughout the Community. Fourth, and most vague, the creation of a monetary union would assist the emergence "of a European reserve currency (and thus) would considerably facilitate international monetary cooperation and a reform of the present system."[11]

Nevertheless, prospective lenders and borrowers are generally not as convinced as economists of the unalterability of exchange rates. Moreover, savers and investors in Europe are not satisfied with the knowledge that their currency will not be devalued in terms of another of the currencies of the Six; they want further assurances against a devaluation of the currency in which the bond is denominated, and sometimes they want even more the added possibility of a financial gain in the event of a general devaluation. Various methods have been used to meet these desires.

1. Gold value clauses have been tried; however, these are risky because they may be unenforceable. Governments have a history of declaring gold clauses legally void or voidable because their enforcement would put the future value of the currency in doubt as well as sanction private regulation of currency value.

2. Many issues are denominated in a confidence-inspiring currency, often the dollar. Another respectable currency is the mark, either by itself or jointly with the dollar. For instance, an Italian state holding, IRI, in 1964 issued 25 million dollars of bonds with the option for subscribers to claim interest and reimbursement either in dollars or in marks. The floating of Swiss Franc bonds outside Switzerland has raised objections from the Swiss authorities, who do not want their currency to be used for transactions outside Switzerland.

3. "The search for ways to attract long-term funds into foreign issues led at one time to the flotation of bonds denominated in European 'units of account.' The issues, with maturities ranging between 15 and 20 years and coupons between 5½ and 6½ per-

[11] For details on the action program, see "Europe's Imbalance," *The Banker* (London), April 1964.

cent, were generally offered in Luxembourg, with a Belgian or Luxembourg bank heading the underwriting syndicate.

"Units of account, which were first used in the bookkeeping of the former European Payments Union, are a composite of seventeen European currencies. They serve as a common denominator for issues floated in several markets and provide a limited guarantee against exchange rate changes for debtors and creditors with liabilities and claims in foreign currencies.

"The unit of account is an entirely artificial yardstick that is used solely to measure the value of contractual loan obligations.

"Since its appearance in early 1961, the unit-of-account formula has taken a number of different forms. It has always provided that the value of the unit would change only if the values of all seventeen reference currencies changed; however, under the terms of the more recent loan agreements at least two thirds of these changes must be in the same direction. Under these conditions, the value of the unit—and hence of the securities denominated in these units— would be adjusted, after a lapse of two years, in the same direction and proportion as the currency among the two thirds (or more) that had changed the least. The protection afforded by this complex formula is of course not absolute. It does not cover the borrower if his currency is devalued, or the lender if his is revalued, vis-à-vis all the others."[12]

4. Parallel loans involve the simultaneous flotation on different national capital markets of different tranches of an issue, with each tranche denominated in the currency of the country where it is placed. Only a few issues have utilized this method. One example is a flotation by an Italian electric company, which issued 6 percent fifteen-year bonds (at various prices) in all the capital markets

---

[12] Federal Reserve Bank of New York, *Recent Innovations in European Capital Markets* (New York, January 1965). The system is described more fully by its main sponsor, F. Collin, in *The Formation of a European Capital Market* (Kredietbank, 1963). See, also, the study by Fédération bancaire de la CEE, *L'utilisation de l'unité de compte dans l'entreprise Européenne* (Brussels, 1966); and Jean L. Blondeel, "A New Form of International Financing: Loans in European Units of Account," *Columbia Law Review*, June 1964.

of the Six; the Belgian share was taken up privately, outside the market.[13]

5. Open-end investment trusts enable the investor to spread his risks among many investments; to lessen the danger of currency devaluations, investments can be made in issues of different currencies. These investment trusts are growing. They are being used more and more to tempt savers into the European long-term capital market, as it becomes increasingly overburdened by European, American, and other capital issues. An example of interest is the new Renta Fund, which plans to invest in a mixture of bonds, shares, and convertible bonds:

An attempt is being made by the Banque de Bruxelles and its partly owned affiliate, the International Bank of Luxemburg, with the launching of the first open-ended fund specializing in foreign currency bond issues. It is known as the Renta Fund and its units will be offered at the equivalent of $56 each. These are intended to appeal to the individual investor who has thus far played only a minimal role in the international bond market, partly because dollar bonds are usually denominated in units of $1000 each. Renta Fund hopes to offer its investors an initial yield of 6%. This would allow it a margin of as much as a full point, especially if it follows its intention of concentrating on securities of sound but unspectacular traditional borrowers in the European market rather than on those of the glamourous American Newcomers.[14]

6. Another method, bonds convertible into shares, is rapidly growing in popularity. For example, SGI International Holdings (an Italian-owned public works and agricultural company) borrowed in Luxembourg 15 million dollars at 6½ percent with two detachable warrants entitling the lender to purchase shares on specific dates. In general, European borrowers have not, as yet, issued many of these convertible debentures, mainly because of legal obstacles. More than a dozen American companies, however, generally acting through subsidiaries created solely for this purpose,

13 One of the main promoters of parallel loans is the German banker; see H. J. Abs, *Le marché Européen de valeurs et d'emissions*, 1964.

14 "Luring the Little Man," *The Economist* (London), May 7, 1966, p. 627.

have successfully floated convertible debentures on the European capital markets in amounts varying between 15 and 50 million dollars.

From the borrower's point of view, individual European or national bond markets may be distinguished from the overall European capital market. Bonds floated in the international European market, rather than the national capital markets, are, of course, usually placed with lenders other than those in the country of issue. It is very difficult to arrive at an overall statistical view of the European bond market. Table 14 reproduces the European Investment Bank's brave attempt to picture this market in 1964. It should be noted that the total amount of bonds sold in the European capital market in 1964 reached about 700 million dollars, of which only about 150 million dollars' worth was purchased through intra-European movements of capital.

In 1967 an important step toward a broad international bond market in Europe was taken when several European and American banks formed an association, "Bondtrade," to provide a clearing mechanism for outstanding Eurodollar bonds. The additional liquidity provided by such a secondary market organization greatly facilitates savings flows across national boundaries.

TABLE 14

Public Issues of Bonds on the So-Called
European Market in 1964
(millions of dollars)

Deutsche Mark or option DM	249
Dollars	437
Units of accounts	10
Total	696

of which there are   149 borrowers from EEC countries
                      326 borrowers from Scandinavia
                      145 borrowers from Japan
                       76 other borrowers

Source: Banque Européenne d'Investissement, *Rapport annuel*, 1965, p. 44.

Savings originating in one of the Six countries can find their way into another of these countries through many channels. Apart from stock exchanges, these include international banking groups or consortia and Community institutions, such as the ECSC High Authority, the European Investment Bank, and the European Social Fund. Long-term loans (arranged between banks, acceptance houses, real estate institutions, equipment leasing companies, and, to a small extent, insurance companies), about which very little information is available, constitute another medium. Finally, the rapidly expanding use of export credits must be mentioned as a channel for the transfer of savings.

When banks are asked to supply more international medium-term credit—and this happens with increasing frequency in Europe, because of the lengthening of some production processes—they themselves usually have to borrow, either immediately or soon after lending. In this situation, banks use one or more of the following techniques, which very often result in a flow of capital across intra-European borders:

1. Borrowing from insurance companies (but these are still accustomed to lending on long or short, not medium, terms).
2. Borrowing from a central bank (if its statutes allow), from special state institutions set up for the purpose, or from state savings institutions.
3. Borrowing from enterprises or individuals who have cash available for one year or more. The German banks, for instance, issue 2- to 3-year "Schuldscheine" (capital notes) bearing between 7 and 8½ percent interest.

E: THE MONEY MARKETS

The Rise in Short-Term Bank Loans

Little official liberalization of capital flows has taken place so far between EEC countries (except for short-term credit linked to trade operations). Nevertheless, a great deal has happened without official guidance.

After World War II and in the early 50's, it was impossible to consider the European money market as a whole. There existed a number of national markets operating independently within the political boundaries of each country and protecting themselves from neighboring markets by extremely strict exchange regulations.

When external payments were finally brought into equilibrium in most of the European countries, the exchange authorities allowed banks to extend their dealings to short-term financial operations in foreign currencies and in foreign markets. These were gradually linked, not only within the Community, but also with the main international centers of New York and London. As a consequence, there is now one vast international short-term money market, with funds flowing freely from one center to another, according to fluctuations in interest rates and the possibilities of exchange risks.

The depth of this international market increases as bank deposits increase, and bank deposits have grown rapidly in most countries. In the Community alone, from 1958 to 1962, bank deposits increased 100 percent in France, 90 percent in Italy, 83 percent in Germany, 80 percent in Holland, and 60 percent in Belgium.[15] The nature of this growth in deposits has also led to credits of longer duration in the international market. The bank deposit increases have been mainly in the form of time deposits (from a week to three or six months, occasionally for even longer periods). This, in turn, has enabled the banks to extend the duration of some credits on the international money market.

The Eurocurrencies

In a number of countries, maximum interest rates on deposits are fixed either as an act of economic policy or by concerted restrictive practices. As a result, funds tend to be deposited in other countries in order to increase their yield. This has given rise to the so-called Eurocurrencies, the best known of which is the Eurodollar.

[15] H. P. Crombe, *The Monetary and Financial Markets in Europe* (Brussels, 1962).

The Eurodollar market has grown in seven years to a network of 400 banks, operating in 25 to 35 countries, and turning over $7 billion of short-term resources. Interest rates in the market are the only short-term rates in Europe that are freely determined by competitive forces; and these forces are so international in scope that no one country, not even the United States, can control them. Interest rates in the Eurodollar market are generally low enough (and they are additionally shaved in tight competitive situations) to be competitive for some transactions in every country and to be competitive for all transactions in many countries. Billions of dollars have been deposited in banks in Canada, the United Kingdom, and continental Western Europe; and the difference between rates of interest paid on these deposits and on comparable assets in the United States has steadily decreased in the last few years. Business enterprises, despite declarations, showed by their transactions that they considered the dollar to be the trading and reserve currency and, as later developments have suggested, the international unit of account. The market in Eurodollars has grown despite misgivings in some quarters since 1958 about the strength of the dollar, and many who have held dollars could not find any better currency in which to hold their assets.

The Eurodollar market has helped to unify short-term capital markets in Europe and suggest how operations based on foreign currencies may affect long-term capital markets; but even if it does not, it has brought a new spirit of competition and expansion to European commercial banking.[16]

Eurodollars are supplied by

- enterprises that want to cover their exchange in advance: they lend to the market the dollars thus obtained until they need them;
- exporters who keep dollars they have earned;
- American residents in search of short-term interest rates higher than those they can obtain at home;
- central banks wishing to invest part of their dollar reserves.

Eurodollars are demanded by

- everyone in search of comparatively cheap short-term loans;

[16] Oscar Altman, "The Integration of European Capital Markets," *The Journal of Finance,* Chicago, May 1965.

- banks that cover themselves in dollars while floating new issues of dollar securities;
- suppliers of Eurodollars who want their money back.

In general, the duration of Eurodollar loans ranges from one day to six months; a few are for nine months or a year. Of course, if renewed, their effective duration can be longer. It is suspected that this renewal procedure has been used in a few cases for long-term finance; however, the practice is limited because it is considered too dangerous by most financiers.

The Eurodollar market makes use of many intermediaries, commissions are sometimes quite small, and the final users are often unknown. According to one of the most comprehensive studies,[17] end uses of Eurodollars cannot be traced statistically in a comprehensive fashion. Table 15, however, makes possible a few broad observations. Of the $13 billion of Eurodollars outstanding at the end of 1966, some $7.1 billion was used outside Western Europe; and of this amount, $4.1 billion was employed in the United States—some $2.3 billion more than in 1965, owing to extraordinarily tight monetary conditions in the United States during the latter half of 1966. For this reason, Eurodollar uses in Western Europe did not increase much in 1966; of more importantce, they did not decline, maintaining their 1965 level of $5 billion in the area including the Common Market countries. The bulk of this amount consisted of accommodations to commercial borrowers resident in the same countries as the banks that extended the loans. This is particularly true in Italy; indeed, of the $4.2 billion domestically outstanding at the end of 1966, as much as $2 billion represented lending by Italian banks to local residents. The importance of the Eurodollar market has become increasingly apparent to official Western European monetary institutions, they being the source of $2.8 billion in 1966, as opposed to only $0.8 billion in 1964.

[17] First National City Bank of New York, *Monthly Economic Letter* (New York, July 1966), pp. 82–83.

TABLE 15

Estimated Sources and Uses of Funds in the Eurodollar Market

(amounts outstanding in billions of dollars)

	Sources			Uses		
	1964	1965	1966	1964	1965	1966
United States	$ 0.7	$ 0.8	$ 1.1	$ 1.5	$ 1.8	$ 4.1
Rest of world outside Western Europe	3.2	3.3	3.0	1.8	2.5	3.0
Western Europe						
EEC countries plus Great Britain, Sweden, and Switzerland of which:	3.3	5.0	6.8	4.3	5.0	5.0
Official monetary institutions	0.8	2.2	2.8	—	—	—
Individuals and businesses resident in the same country as the reporting banks	1.7	1.8	2.5	3.8	4.4	4.2
Residents of other countries than the reporting banks	0.8	1.0	1.5	0.5	0.6	0.8
All other Western European countries	0.8	0.9	2.1	0.4	0.7	0.9
Total Western Europe	4.1	5.9	8.9	4.7	5.7	5.9
Grand Total	8.0	10.0	13.0	8.0	10.0	13.0

Source: Adapted from the Bank for International Settlements, *Thirty-Seventh Annual Report, June 12, 1967.*

F: THE LEGAL AND INSTITUTIONAL POSITION
REGARDING INTRA-EUROPEAN CAPITAL FLOWS

An Institutional Classification of Capital Flows

National accounting and balance-of-payments statistics are useful in obtaining a picture of capital flows, but a realistic appraisal of the extent and future of liberalization in this area also requires an analysis of legal and institutional positions. The classification presently used by the civil servants (mainly in central banks) who are in charge of imposing or removing restrictions and also by Common Market authorities (with very slight amendments) is that given in Annex D to the OECD "Code of Liberalisation of Capital Movements."[18]

Table 16, picturing the present degree of liberalization, uses the OECD system of classification. However, in order to simplify the table, capital flows are shown as such without distinction between capital exports and capital imports, and a few of the OECD subheadings are condensed.

The EEC Directives (For pre-EEC efforts to liberalize capital movements, see Appendix II.)

As indicated in the second column of Table 16, the EEC Council has approved two directives implementing Article 67 of the Rome Treaty and calling for the removal of certain national restrictions on capital movements within the Community.[19]

When the first directive was issued in May 1960, Germany, Belgium, and Luxembourg were not required to take any further liberalization measures since their capital-control regulations were already sufficiently liberal. France, Italy, and the Netherlands, however, had to take certain steps; of course, they agreed to these

[18] Paris, June 1965.
[19] See Section B of this chapter, p. 44, for Article 67 and accompanying provisions of the Rome Treaty.

measures because, under Article 69, at this stage in the Community's evolution approval of the directive by the Council had to be unanimous. The second directive, approved in December 1962, supplemented and slightly amended the first directive to provide increased liberalization of capital flows.

In general, the directives oblige the member states to permit capital transfers for certain operations to be effected on the free exchange markets. More specifically, member states must authorize capital transfers for direct investments, real estate transactions, certain credit and surety transactions, and transfers of private funds for personal purposes. In addition to authorizing the transfers, the member states must guarantee that the exchange rates for these transfers will not substantially differ from the rate of exchange for current transactions (which deviates no more than one percent from par value). The directives also require general authorization of free capital movements for many important transactions in securities. For these generally authorized transfers, the member states are not obliged to guarantee a rate of exchange close to par; they are directed only to endeavor to provide such a rate.

Certain types of dealing in securities, such as the issue or placing of securities on the capital markets and the acquisition of securities not quoted on stock exchanges, are exempted from the order for general authorization if national restrictions existed at the time that the first directive became effective. For these capital movements the directives lay down conditional liberalization in that a member state is able to retain or re-establish the restrictions if abolition would hinder the achievement of its economic objectives. France, Italy, and the Netherlands have informed the Commission, pursuant to this exemption, of their intention to maintain, as a whole or in part, the restrictions in force.[20] However, a co-operative desire for progress in this area was immediately exhibited when the Netherlands Government authorized more foreign security

[20] Commission, European Economic Community, *Fourth General Report on the Activities of the Community* (Brussels, 1961).

TABLE 16

State of the Liberalization of Intra-European Capital Movements at the Beginning of 1966

Type of Capital Investments	Liberalized by First and Second Council Directives	To Be Liberalized When the Third Council Directive Comes into Force	To Be Liberalized at a Later Stage
I. Direct investment (investment for the purpose of establishing lasting economic relations with an undertaking, in particular, investments that give the possibility of exercising an effective influence on the management thereof) by means of	x		
1. Creation or extension of a wholly owned enterprise, subsidiary, or branch, or acquisition of full ownership of an existing enterprise			
2. Participation in a new or existing enterprise			
3. A long-term loan (5 years and longer)			
II. Liquidation of direct investment	x		
III. Admission of securities (shares or bonds) to capital markets			
1. Issue through placing or public sale		x	
2. Introduction on a recognized foreign security exchange		x	

IV. Buying and selling of securities			
1–2. Purchase and sale on a recognized security exchange of listed securities, excluding open-end investment trusts	x (partly)	x (partly)	
3–4. Purchase and sale of unlisted securities or open-end investment trusts			x
V. Operations in real estate		x	
VI. Buying and Selling of short-term treasury bills and other short-term securities normally dealt in on the money market			x
VII. Credits directly linked with international commercial transactions or with the rendering of international services			
i. In cases where a resident participates in the underlying commercial or service transaction			
Credits granted:			
1. Short-term (less than 1 year)		x	
2. Medium-term (from 1 to 5 years)		x	
3. Long-term (5 years and longer)			
ii. In cases where no resident participates in the underlying commercial or service transaction			
Credits granted:			
1. Short-term			x
2. Medium-term			x
3. Long-term			x
VIII. Financial credits and loans			x

TABLE 16 (Continued)

Type of Capital Investments	Liberalized by First and Second Council Directives	To Be Liberalized When the Third Council Directive Comes into Force	To Be Liberalized at a Later Stage
IX. Operation of accounts with credit institutions			x
X. Personal capital movements			
A. Loans			x
B. Gifts and endowments	x		
C. Dowries	x		
D. Inheritances and legacies	x		
E. Settlement of debts in their country of origin by immigrants	x		
F. Emigrants' assets	x		
G. Savings of nonresident workers	x		
H, I, L, M. Miscellaneous	x		
XI. Life insurance	Linked to the operations concerned		x
XII. Sureties and guarantees			
XIII. Physical movement of capital assets			
A. Securities and other documents of title to capital assets			x
B. Nonindustrial gold	x		
XIV. Miscellaneous	x (with some exceptions)		

issues in 1962, and three loans were floated in the same year on the Italian market by international financial institutions.[21] France, on the other hand, is only now beginning to hint that it will allow foreign flotations on its capital markets.

A third directive was proposed by the Commission in April 1964 but was not approved by the Council until February 1967. This directive eliminates certain legal and/or administrative obstacles to the issue and placing of foreign securities on national capital markets, to the introduction of foreign securities on national stock exchanges, and to the acquisition of foreign securities by financial institutions.[22] The reasons for the long delay in approval of the third directive are examined in Section H of this chapter.

In summation, there are, at present, only three instances in which capital can flow among the Six with complete freedom:

1. Personal capital movements and investments without intermediaries, which the member states agreed to liberalize for the following reasons: all such investments can be easily verified by the national authorities; these investments are sometimes necessary to ensure adequate supplies of raw materials for national industries; direct investments by enterprises are very closely tied to the philosophy of competition within the Common Market; and investments in real estate and personal capital movements are linked to personal freedom.

2. Short-term capital movements arising out of commercial transactions in which a resident of the Common Market participates, provided the credit is granted for less than five years. This was allowed, indeed almost necessitated, as a natural extension of the free movement of goods.

3. Transactions in securities quoted on a stock exchange in a Common Market country (subject to a number of administrative annoyances in France and Italy, and excluding open-end invest-

---

[21] Commission, European Economic Community, *Sixth General Report on the Activities of the Community* (Brussels, 1963).

[22] Commission, European Economic Community, *Eighth General Report on the Activities of the Community* (Brussels, 1965).

ment trusts). Liberalization in this area was probably granted as a token of good will by the otherwise overcautious national authorities.

Nonliberalized Capital Flows

OBJECTIVES.[23] The objectives—sometimes avowed, sometimes hidden—of some national governments, when refusing to liberalize all intra-European capital flows, appear in Table 17. They are, in order of diminishing importance, as follows.

1. Improvement in the balance of payments. Countries fear a loss of reserves either at a particular moment or at some later time. With reference to Table 17, this has been the reason for not liberalizing items VI (short-term treasury bills), VII.i.3. and VII.ii (some types of commercial credit), and VIII (financial credit) of the OECD list in France, Italy, and possibly the Netherlands. In France, there has been the additional goal of accumulating large gold reserves, a national monetary policy pursued with peculiar resolve.

2. Price stability. This objective, dear to the hearts of central bankers (and thus requiring lip service by the financial community), can be threatened by

- too high interest rates, if one believes in the cost-push variety of inflation: this consideration explains restrictions on outward capital flows in Belgium;
- too large a surplus in the current balance of payments, if one subscribes to the theory of demand-pull inflation: this belief leads to action against inward capital flows, in order to avoid an excessive influx of gold and/or excessive liquidity in the home money market. Such action has been taken in Germany[24] and to a small extent in France and the Netherlands.

---

[23] This survey draws on Fédération bancaire de la CEE, *Note du professeur Meinberg sur la libération des mouvements de capitaux* (Brussels, 1965).

[24] "Problèmes d'inflation et mouvements de capitaux," *Bulletin hebdomadaire de la Kredietbank* (Brussels, May 23, 1964).

3. Protection of particular industries, which is often achieved by giving them priority access to capital markets. For this reason, outward flows tend to be checked in the Netherlands, France, and particularly Italy.

4. The satisfaction of collective needs. This is the main concern of finance ministers, who are often short of current revenue and thus compelled to borrow in order to finance current expenditures. By preventing outward capital flows, the Belgian Government reserves "as large a share of the market as possible for its own issues."[25]

5. The protection of small savers from the vicissitudes of international finance. Because of this universal objective, all countries are very careful with unlisted securities (item IV.3.4. in the OECD classification), limit access to their stock exchanges, and keep a close eye on the foreign investments of insurance companies and savings institutions. The result is a check on outward flows. This wariness is particularly evident for new types of capital flows, such as the open-end investment trusts.

6. Facilitation of income distribution improvements. Efforts in this direction are made more difficult by the movement of capital in search of tax advantages. This reasoning is behind restrictions on outward flows in countries where the tax-haven temptations provided by the Luxembourg Government are especially strong, that is, Belgium, France, and Italy.

7. Miscellaneous items of economic policy, not always rational. Capital movements may be impeded for reasons that the economist does not rank as objectives, but that still carry great weight with ministers and administrations. This category includes

- the desire in finance ministries not to change existing taxes, even if they prevent outward or inward capital movements, because "an old tax is a good tax";
- the wish in foreign affairs ministries not to change bilateral agreements arrived at after painful negotiations, especially

[25] See Crombe, *The Monetary and Financial Markets in Europe,* Brussels, 1962.

when parliamentary ratification of treaties is involved: this reason was given by the Netherlands to justify retention of certain discriminatory taxes;

- the pursuit of reciprocity, which is one reason why the Belgian, German, and Luxembourg governments will not lift certain restrictions on outward capital movements until the other three countries agree to do the same;
- the fear that capital movements outward may jeopardize the financing of particular investments that the economic planners consider important.

INSTRUMENTS. The objectives just discussed are the causes of capital flow restrictions. The restrictions themselves, which con-

TABLE 17

Nonliberalized Intra-European Capital Flows

Category in OECD Classification	*Main Objectives*
III. Admission of securities to bond markets	Protection of small savers
	Priority to national government requirements (i.e., collective needs)
	Protection to particular industries
IV.3.4. Purchase and sale of open-end investment trust and of unlisted securities	Protection of small savers
	Prevention of tax evasion
VI. Buying and selling of short-term treasury bills and other short-term securities	Balance of payments
	Price stability
VII.i.3. Credits linked to commercial transactions, long term	Balance of payments
VII.ii. Credits linked to commercial transactions involving no resident	Balance of payments
	Price stability
VIII. Financial credit and loans	Balance of payments
	Price stability
IX. Operation of accounts with credit institutions	Uncertain

stitute the instruments whereby the governments of the Six attempt to reach these objectives, can be divided into four general categories: direct controls, credit restrictions, taxes, and institutional impediments.

Direct Controls.—Exchange control is, of course, the main instrument affecting intra-European capital movements. According to Segre:

Restrictions placed on capital movements of a monetary character by the exchange regulations of various countries have in reality lost much of their importance owing to the development of the Euro-dollar and other "external" markets for the major Western currencies; even in countries with relatively restricted exchange freedom, like Italy, the authorities have allowed through this expedient the formation of a close and effective link between the national money market and the international markets.

Exchange controls, however, continue to present an undeniably important obstacle in transactions of a more "financial" character— in particular, the issue of foreign bonds and the granting of long and medium term loans to foreign residents (as well as the reverse operations). These transactions are still subject to the "conditional" liberalisation specified in the first directive, i.e. that freeing is not obligatory where the movement of capital threatens to impede the attainment of the aims of the economic policy of a Member State.

It is important to note that, in this respect, the function assumed by exchange control regulations is not their normal one, which is the safeguarding of the balance of payments equilibrium from large unforeseen destabilising capital movements: the employment of exchange control regulations to restrict foreign issues or credits, in order to maintain equilibrium in domestic capital and money markets, is in fact revealed as an instrument of domestic monetary policy.[26]

Dividend control has a nuisance value; however, it is rarely used nowadays in continental Europe.

Access to capital markets can involve many forms of discrimination against foreign borrowers. Such access is regulated in each

[26] C. Segre, *Financial Markets in the E.E.C.—Prospects for Integration* (Moorgate and Wall Street, autumn 1963), pp. 44–45.

of the Common Market countries, Germany being the most permissive and France the most restrictive.[27] Although this control is meant to protect small savers, it is, in fact, preventing or limiting the issue of shares and bonds by nonresident enterprises.

Access to the stock exchanges is often made more difficult for foreign enterprises through various seemingly respectable devices. This has been the case in Italy and particularly in France for open-end investment trusts.[28]

Credit Restrictions.—Limitations on lending by nonbanking institutions are frequently mentioned as an obstacle to intra-European capital movements. On this point Segre states:

Finally particular attention must be paid to regulations concerning the investment policies of institutional investors (insurance companies, savings banks, pension funds, etc. . . .) in respect of their collected funds, and in particular their reserves. While it is true that the regulations governing the investment policies of such institutions are principally designed to protect the policy-holders or depositors, they also have in practice the effect of creating a market reserved for a few privileged borrowers, such as the government, local authorities, and other semigovernment organisations.

Obviously certain controls, instituted with a view of ensuring the stability of financial markets and the protection of savings, require exercise of discretion in particular cases. However, it has to be recognized that the absence of clearly specified criteria upon which such decisions are based frequently puts foreign issuers in a particularly difficult situation, partly because they are not sufficiently knowledgeable about the administrative practice of the country concerned, and partly because the decisions taken are of a discriminatory character, which, although expressly forbidden by the Rome Treaty, is sometimes difficult to prove.[29]

Directives to banking institutions and approval of individual loans can also play nefarious roles when banks are directed by the authorities not to lend to foreigners.

[27] For details, see R. Larcier, *La Revue de la Banque* (Brussels), No. 1, 1959, pp. 65–67.
[28] For details, see "La circulation des capitaux dans le Marché Commun," *Le Crédit du Nord* (Lille, 1963), pp. 22–34.
[29] See Segre, *Financial Markets in the E.E.C.*, pp. 45–46.

Government loans and guarantees of loans to national enterprises are a subtle means of discriminating between borrowers and hence an instrument preventing or restricting free capital movements. These practices are widespread, despite the Rome Treaty clauses expressly forbidding this type of government subsidization.

Taxes.—Stamp duties on securities and taxes on stock exchange transactions differ from country to country, and until they are harmonized, the integration of capital markets will be hindered. Duties on securities are levied in Germany (3 percent), in Belgium (1.6 percent), and in the Netherlands (2 percent). Stock exchange transactions are taxed everywhere except in Luxembourg. For instance, as of June 1966, cash transactions on shares were taxed as follows:

Germany	0.225 percent
Belgium	0.250
France	0.600
Italy at least	0.005
the Netherlands at least	0.129

Taxes on income from bonds and shares differ considerably from country to country and may be levied twice on a receiver of foreign income (in the country of the enterprise and in his own country) unless a double-taxation treaty is in force. In theory, there should be fifteen such agreements among the Six; in fact, there are only five: between Belgium and France (the only recent one); and between Italy, on the one hand, and Belgium, France, Germany, and Luxembourg, on the other hand.

Of course, harmonization of taxes and elimination of double taxation raise very complicated issues, far beyond the integration of capital markets. Nevertheless, the present situation is a major obstacle to that end and an incentive to large-scale tax evasion.

Institutional Impediments.—Company laws and other institutional requirements vary among the Six to such an extent as to provide a significant restriction on capital flow. The need for their harmonization or, in the alternative, supersedence by European laws raises many issues apart from capital market integration. Those issues most related to financial integration are discussed in Chapter 4.

G: POSSIBLE NONGOVERNMENTAL ACTIONS
PROMOTING CAPITAL FLOWS

European integration is influenced not only by Community institutions and national governments; much progress in financial integration can also be made through the efforts of private economic institutions. There are many proposals for actions on the part of these groups, but only the four proposals that appear most likely to succeed in the near future will be discussed here.

Adequate Disclosure by Security Issuers

European companies are much more secretive than their American counterparts. This lack of candor makes it difficult for them to tap savings, especially in countries other than their own.

At present, laws in Europe require no more than annual reports, and many companies go no further than this legal minimum, for fear of giving away information to competitors, trade unions, customers, suppliers, or various tax collectors.[30] Official statistics and the financial press cannot contribute much more than what the companies make available to the public. Banks and a few official bodies may have more information, but it is not available to the general public.

Possible progress in this area may be made along the lines proposed by the International Federation of Stock Exchanges, which has announced that it would like to obtain, if possible on a quarterly basis, balance sheets (consolidated for groups if need be), operating accounts, financial results, and comments on current activities.

---

[30] For a summary description of legal requirements, see Larcier, *La Revue de la Banque*, pp. 68–70.

More Flexible Investment by Institutional Investors

Segre states:

For financial institutions the problem is the traditional one, namely that undertakings in domestic currency towards depositors or policy holders must be represented by assets realisable in the same currency. The logic underlying this principle is clearly to prevent financial institutions taking exchange risks: but to put this in proportion it should be noted that, where these institutions are allowed to hold ordinary shares, the fluctuations to which they thereby are exposed are at least as dangerous as the risks that are incurred by holding bonds expressed in a foreign currency. It seems that it might well be opportune therefore to soften this principle somewhat.[31]

Relatively little interest is exhibited by European investment institutions in nongovernment securities. One of the reasons, of course, is the control placed on these institutions (for instance, the legal list of permissible investments). Another reason is tradition; the habits or policies of these institutions do not necessitate broader investment (for example, few insurance policies are tied to a cost-of-living index, and therefore insurance companies need not hedge against inflation). A third, very important reason, which is often overlooked, is the simple fact that only a limited choice of first-class securities is available to the institutional investor in his country. This limitation of choice is especially apparent in a small country such as Belgium, where the number of securities issued by individual companies may be large but the number of companies is quite small. With the rapid growth of major industrial and especially manufacturing companies, both the national institutional investor and the national enterprises are outgrowing the limitations of their national capital markets, and this situation leads to more capital flows across national boundaries.

This "Europeanization" of portfolios could result in an overall increase in the resources available for bond and equity financing.

[31] See Segre, *Financial Markets in the E.E.C.*, p. 49. This treatment is further expanded by A. Lamfalussy, *Towards a European Capital Market*, lecture at a conference on international monetary problems, London 1965.

Insurance company A in Belgium may be reluctant to add to its holdings of bonds or shares issued by Belgian manufacturing company X since these holdings are already quite large in relation to its total investments; yet it might consider an investment in the securities of French Company Y. Conversely, French insurance company B may be prepared to add to its portfolio the shares of the Belgian manufacturer, whereas it would hesitate to invest more heavily in the French Company Y.

Rationalization Moves by Stock Exchanges

Although, as we have already seen in Section D, European stock exchanges are very small and very jealous of each other, a number of things can be done to encourage freer capital movements. Among the possibilities, several appear probable, such as unifying time periods for term contracts, unifying and simplifying stock exchange procedures, and, particularly, setting up a European system whereby securities could be bought and sold without actually being mailed, as is done at present, between one center and another. The French have established such a system for their country,[32] and proposals have been made at a European level.[33] However, a serious difficulty is presented by the desire of Europeans for bearer securities that facilitate the evasion of income taxes and death duties.

One answer suggested to this problem is the creation of a "Caisse de Virements," which would act as a nominee and take charge of foreign securities handled in a registered form. Thus, the costly issue of bearer certificates would be avoided, except for holders willing to pay the extra price.

Extension of Bank Networks

So far, most European banks are content to function in their

[32] L. Averan-Horteur, *De la C.C.D.V.T. à la SICOVAN* (Paris, Dalloz, 1959).

[33] R. Dewaay, "Circulation des valeurs mobilières entre les pays du Marché Commun," *Les bourses de valeurs mobilières dans le Marché Commun* (Brussels, 1958).

home countries, and foreign subsidiaries are only minor affairs. However, American banks are now doing good business, through large agencies, in most Common Market countries, and their example will certainly give rise either to full mergers between banks of different nationalities or to the creation of very close relationships between members of syndicates, though each one would retain its identity. The latter alternative is the more popular at present, but in the long run the precedent of industrial and commercial mergers is likely to be followed by the more conservative bankers.

H: POSSIBLE GOVERNMENT ACTIONS FAVORING A UNIFIED CAPITAL MARKET

There appears to be a chance that Europe will have a unified capital market by the end of 1970. It would be quite small by American standards and perhaps isolated to some extent from the capital markets of the rest of the world. Also, it is likely to exist *de facto* before the resistance of cautious civil servants is finally overcome. The three main policy instruments that will be involved are exchange controls, indirect taxes affecting stock exchanges, and direct taxation of interests and dividends.

Exchange Controls and Stock Exchange Regulations

As discussed earlier in this chapter, the first two directives, implementing Article 67 of the Rome Treaty, completely liberalized some capital flows and also provided limited or conditional liberalization in four cases:

1. Purchase and sale of unlisted securities and open-end investment trusts.[34]
2. Long-term (i.e., five years or longer) credits linked to commercial transactions in which a resident participates.[35]
3. Medium- and long-term (i.e., one year or longer) credits

[34] OECD category IV.3.4; see Table 17.
[35] OECD category VII.i.3; see Table 17.

linked to a commercial operation, but in which no resident participates.[36]

4. Financial credits and loans.[37]

Yearly reports are being made on these categories to the EEC Commission by the member states. Difficulties have arisen in France, Italy, and the Netherlands, but gradual solutions now being found foretell eventual complete liberalization in these areas.

As we have already seen in Section F of this chapter, the EEC Council has approved a third directive toward the liberalization of capital movements. Items liberalized are the issuance of securities through placing and public sale, their introduction on stock exchanges, and the placing of foreign securities with savings institutions.

Although the directive was proposed by the Commission in April 1964, it was not approved by the Council until February 1967, because of the extremely cautious attitudes of the finance ministries in France, Italy, and the Netherlands. This dilatory stance was partly the result of a desire not to compromise national economic policy objectives by further sacrificing potential exchange controls and other restrictive devices.

Despite this hesitancy, a solution was found, using the technique of gradualness that has succeeded in other fields: access to national capital markets will be allowed by the three recalcitrant countries in increasing amounts each year. Belgium and Germany, which were willing to liberalize immediately but insisted on reciprocity, will join in the gradual process. Luxembourg, of course, has been extremely liberal for many years; however, the funds lent on its capital market come from everywhere in the world.

Disagreements as to what constitutes reciprocity led the Commission, pursuant to Article 155 of the Rome Treaty, to issue in April, 1968, an opinion and recommendation concerning the

[36] OECD category VII.ii; see Table 17.
[37] OECD category VIII; see Table 17.

implementation of the third directive. This interpretation upheld the powers of national officials to authorize capital flotations, while, at the same time, insisting that this discretion not be used to discriminate in favor of nationals or to define reciprocity in terms of capital flows.

Indirect Taxes Affecting Stock Exchanges

Efforts have been made since 1962 toward a new directive "harmonizing and bringing into line methods for the collection and assessment of taxes on issues and transfers of securities."[38] Germany poses a problem in this area because of a conflict between the federal government and the states as to their respective powers of taxation. Another obstacle is the fact that Luxembourg, a corporate haven prospering from franchise fees, wants to avoid any tax system based on the legal seat of companies.

Taxation of Interest and Dividends

Income from property held in one country by a resident of another country is likely to be taxed twice, that is, in each of the two countries. For this reason and others, tax evasion in the country of residence is frequent (it is often impossible in the country where the property is held, because taxes are usually deducted at the source). Aside from the problem of tax evasion and the question of fairness, it is contrary to the concept of a unified capital market to have citizens paying higher taxes on their foreign investments than on their home investments.

In the past, this problem was nearly always tackled at bilateral meetings regularly organized by tax authorities for a general exchange of information. Consequently, double taxation did not usually receive priority attention; as mentioned earlier in this chapter, of the fifteen possible bilateral conventions among the Six, about half are satisfactory. Lately, however, experts have found it

[38] Commission, European Economic Community, *Memorandum on the Action Program of the Community for the Second Stage* (Brussels, 1962).

useful to discuss the double-taxation problem separately, in a multilateral setting; as a result a draft bilateral convention has been written by the OECD.[39]

Encouraged by this example, the EEC Commission has decided to propose implementation of Article 220 of the Rome Treaty: "Member States shall, in so far as necessary, enter into negotiations with each other with a view to ensuring for the benefit of their nationals, the abolition of double taxation with the Community." As part of its proposal, the Commission is preparing a multilateral draft convention having somewhat greater coverage than the OECD bilateral convention and giving priority to the elimination of any tax obstacle preventing unification of capital markets. The member states that will be most seriously concerned with the convention are Belgium, where tax evasion is high, and Luxembourg, which is in no hurry to surrender the benefits derived from being a tax haven.

---

[39] "Projet de convention de double imposition concernant le revenu et la fortune," *Rapport du Comité fiscal de l'O.C.D.E.* (Paris, 1963).

4

THE CREATION OF
NEW FINANCIAL
INSTITUTIONS

A: THE PRECEDENT OF THE EUROPEAN COAL AND
STEEL COMMUNITY (ECSC)

The Paris Treaty[1]

While the Rome Treaty was being drafted, its authors were able
to draw on the experience of the ECSC, which, as mentioned in
Chapter 1, had been established in Paris in 1950 and had been
in operation since 1953. The main supranational body of the
ECSC, it will be recalled, is the High Authority. According to
Article 49 of the Paris Treaty:

The High Authority is empowered to procure the funds necessary to
the accomplishment of its mission:
  by placing levies on the production of coal and steel;
  by borrowing.

Article 50 provides, among other things, that:

The levies are intended to cover:
  the administrative expenses;

---

[1] The quoted parts of the Paris Treaty have been slightly simplified for
purposes of presentation.

the nonreimbursable assistance, relating to re-adaptation;[2]
expenditures to encourage technical and economic research.
The levies shall be assessed annually on the various products according to their average value; however, the rate of the levy may not exceed one percent.

The most important provision in the Paris Treaty for our purposes is Article 51:

1. The funds obtained by borrowing may be used by the High Authority only to grant loans.
   The issuing of bonds by the High Authority on the stock markets of member States shall be subject to the regulations in effect on these markets.
2. The High Authority may guarantee loans granted directly to enterprises by third parties.

The purpose of Article 51 is to provide coal and steel enterprises with more favorable access to capital markets, that is, more abundant credit or credit at a lower rate of interest.

This purpose is spelled out in Article 54:

The High Authority may facilitate the carrying out of investment programs by granting loans to enterprises or by giving its guarantee to other loans which they obtain.

With the unanimous agreement of the Council, the High Authority may by the same means assist the financing of works and installations which contribute directly and mainly to an increase of production or to lower production costs or which facilitate the marketing of products subject to its jurisdiction.

The Financial Operations of the ECSC

The financial operations of the ECSC constitute a success story:

[2] The readaptation provision was extended in 1959: "Should profound changes in the marketing conditions . . . make it necessary for certain enterprises permanently to discontinue, curtail or change their activities, the High Authority may, at the request of the interested Governments (in addition to the granting of nonrepayable assistance) facilitate the financing of programs for the creation of new and economically sound activities, or for the conversion of enterprises, which are capable of assuring productive re-employment to workers rendered redundant" [H. D. Lundstrom, *Capital Movements and Economic Integration* (Leyden, Sythoff, 1961), p. 149].

borrowing at comparatively low rates, lending to deserving enterprises, and being reimbursed by them according to schedule.

The levy on coal and steel enterprises yielded approximately 400 million dollars from 1953 to the end of August 1965.[3] Of this amount, German enterprises provided slightly less than one half and French enterprises slightly less than one quarter.

The ratio of the levy to the value of production was gradually increased by July 1953 to 0.9 percent, stayed at that level for two years, and then went down, in five steps, to 0.2 percent in July 1962; after three years at that level, it rose slightly to the current 0.25 percent. Present yields are approximately 25 million dollars per year, of which three fourths is paid by the steel industry.

The purpose of the relatively high levy rate in the first years was to build up a guaranty fund of 100 million dollars, which would facilitate borrowing in the capital markets; the full amount was reached in 1956. In addition, a special reserve, now reaching 67 million dollars, has been accumulated from sources other than the levy and borrowings, in order to finance the construction of houses for workers.

Borrowing began with a 100 million dollar loan, at a rate of 3⅞ percent, from the United States Export-Import Bank. On this occasion, the High Authority entered into an Act of Pledge, an open-end indenture with the Bank for International Settlements acting as depositary, in order to supplement the protection afforded its lenders by its taxing power and its guaranty fund.[4] Fifteen other loans (four of which have been entirely reimbursed) were contracted under the Act of Pledge in the United States, Belgium, Luxembourg, the Saarland (still under French occupation at the time), the Netherlands, and Switzerland.[5]

---

[3] U. J. Vaes, *Rapport du Commissaire aux comptes de la C.E.C.A. relatif au treizième exercice financier* (Luxembourg, 1965), p. 18.

[4] H. Skribanovitz, "Financial Operations of the E.C.S.C.," in *International Financing and Investment*, edited by J. F. McDaniels (New York, Oceana Publications, 1964), pp. 263–264.

[5] Bank of International Settlements, *36th Annual Report* (Basel, 1966).

After its financial status became firmly established on the market, the ECSC was able to borrow outside the Act of Pledge. At the end of June 1965, total borrowing had reached 560 million dollars, of which 480 million was outstanding (190 million within the Act of Pledge and 290 million outside it). The funds were obtained in the United States (176 million), in Switzerland (23 million), and in all six Common Market countries (Germany, with 105 million, and Luxembourg, with 56 million, being the main lenders). The most expensive terms were approximately 6¼ percent.

Outstanding loans to coal and steel enterprises reached 150 and 256 million dollars, respectively, at the end of June 1965, plus 36 million dollars for workers' houses and 27 million dollars for the reconversion of enterprises.

The High Authority's contribution to any individual project on the average amounts to about twenty-five percent of the total cost, with local banks contributing another twenty-five percent and the remainder being financed from internal resources of the enterprise. This conduct of financial activities across the frontiers of many countries has necessitated a great deal of planning, coordination and adaptation to the different financial and legal systems prevailing in the different countries. Out of this work gradually—and generally unnoticed by the public—some sort of financial integration is developing.

The loans to enterprises have always been made in the same currency as the related funds borrowed by the High Authority so that there has been no exchange risk for the High Authority. The foreign exchange needed to service the loans raised is covered by currency undertakings of Government or Central Banks in those countries which have not yet reached full convertibility of their currencies.

Further, I would like to mention that the High Authority is relending the borrowed funds at cost; it is not necessary to take a margin to cover the credit risk as that risk is already covered by the High Authority's taxing power and the Guaranty Fund. The loans to the enterprises are secured in substantially the same way as might be loans obtained by them from their local banks.[6]

[6] See Skribanovitz in *International Financing and Investment,* pp. 264–265.

The main borrowers from the High Authority are enterprises in Germany (225 million dollars) and Italy (111 million dollars). The latter country has been the main beneficiary of the ECSC's financial operations; its enterprises have obtained more than twice the amount contributed by them for the levy (30 million dollars) and by their financial market (24 million dollars). Table 18 shows, for each of the ECSC countries, the total amount of loans obtained from the ECSC (including the amounts already reimbursed) in relation to the country's total investment in the coal and steel industries during the period 1963–1965.

The High Authority also deposits its liquid assets in several major commercial banks, with the understanding that these funds will be re-lent to coal or steel enterprises. As a consequence, Table 18 understates the effective financial contribution of the ECSC.

TABLE 18

*Share of Community Coal and Steel Investments
Financed by the ECSC*

Country	Total Investment in Coal and Steel in 1963–1965 (million dollars)[a]	Approximate Amount of Loans Received from ECSC in 1963–1965 (million dollars)[b]	Share of Investment Financed by ECSC (%)
Germany	1760	110	6
Belgium	510	10	2
France	840	40	5
Italy	1230	90	7
Luxembourg	100	—	—
Netherlands	190	—	—
Total	4630	280	6

[a] *Les investissements dans les industries du charbon et de l'acier de la Communauté C.E.C.A.*, Rapports sur l'enquête 1965 (July 1965) et sur l'enquête 1966 (July 1966).
[b] Vaes, *Rapport aux comptes de la C.E.C.A.*, p. 63.

At the end of June 1965, guarantees granted by the ECSC on loans contracted by enterprises with third parties stood at 42 million dollars, that is, 9 percent of the amount lent directly.[7]

B: THE EUROPEAN INVESTMENT BANK (EIB)

The EIB was envisioned in the Spaak Report as an investment fund. Its creation was largely the result of requests by the Italian delegates, who stressed the investment problems of their country, particularly those of the South, which had remained comparatively underdeveloped.

Purposes[8]

"To foster the conditions in which the Common Market can develop smoothly and harmoniously, it would appear indispensable to set up an Investment Fund endowed with guaranteed resources and capable of operating as a first-rate borrower in European and international markets. It should furthermore cooperate with other international financial institutions, namely the International Bank for Reconstruction and Development.

"Its first task of course will be to *participate in the financing of projects* which, by their scope or simply by their nature, do not lend themselves easily to the various methods of financing available in each individual State. The most typical projects in this respect would be those involving means of communication and the production or transportation of power, bearing in mind that, under the Coal and Steel Community, investments in the coal industry are financed separately. Particularly heavy calls on the Investment Fund would have to be anticipated for certain nuclear energy projects, quite apart from the burdens or subsidies borne directly by the joint Euratom budget.

[7] See Vaes, *Rapport aux comptes de la C.E.C.A.*, p. 77.
[8] Secretariat of the Intergovernmental Committee Created by the Messina Conference, *Report from the Delegation Heads to the Ministers of Foreign Affairs*, 120 F/56 (mimeographed document, Brussels, 1956).

"It is conceivable that the financial participation of an Investment Fund would increase apace with the European character of each project: this European character would be proven by the number of States involved in or associated with the project, and also by the favorable support or initiative of the relevant European institutions.

"*Joint development of the more backward regions,* such as exist in all the member countries, is a fundamental condition for the success of the Common Market. It is wrong to suggest that, when areas which have not attained the same stage of economic development are suddenly joined together, the lower cost of manpower and the higher return on investment automatically ensure faster progress of the initially less developed region, leading ultimately to the alignment of economic levels. On the contrary, as shown by the Italian unification experiment after 1860, and also in the United States after the War of Secession, the gap may widen cumulatively if the basic conditions for increased production are not first created by public means, that is, a network of roads, ports, and methods of communication, drainage, irrigation and soil improvement programs, schools, and hospitals. Positive and collective action, on the other hand, benefits the more developed areas too, for they share in the enhanced economic activity thus created, and it prevents the pressure on their wages and standard of living which the connection with less developed regions might otherwise entail.

"It would be difficult to overestimate the importance of the part the Investment Fund should play in this field, for the success of the entire European venture. Regular financing is as important as the size of the amounts involved. Accelerated development always affects the balance of payments. Consequently, although the fund's contributions should be used for actual investments and not to cover an external deficit, they tend automatically to solve balance-of-payments problems as well. Although the use of foreign capital to finance economic development does not necessarily entail the import of capital goods, the fact remains that these financial resources facilitate the sale of equipment by countries in which this industry represents a vital link in the productive structure and help to maintain the pace of expansion. Lastly, the creation of employment eliminates the major obstacle of unemployment, which previously hindered the liberalization of manpower resources.

"Agriculture in particular will benefit from regional development plans, since they will enable it to attain greater productivity. And to a certain extent the creation of other activities will solve the problem of certain agricultural sectors whose survival is justified solely by the fact that those employed in them would not find alternative employment.

"To ensure continuity of employment in increasingly productive forms, to facilitate progressive adjustment to the Common Market, to make the best possible use of existing resources, and to reduce, as far as possible, the cost of unavoidable changes, *reconversion* constitutes a vital factor of Common Market policy. It is not enough for increased outlets and competition to incite the appropriate reorientation of activities or changes in production methods. In addition, enterprises which have to effect conversion must be able to find the means thereto. This policy is not only humane, since it helps to prevent the closing of enterprises and the dismissal of manpower, and aims instead to provide alternative employment on the spot: it is also the most economical policy, since it means that full use is made of existing means of production, of the housing, communication, and distribution facilities which gravitate around productive enterprises.

"Thus reconversion and the *creation of new activities* capable of providing productive employment for manpower are among the most socially useful operations: their productivity should be gauged not only by their direct impact or by the fact that they use or save existing facilities, but also by the progressive atmosphere they help to bring about.

"The Fund's contribution need not cover the whole of a project or expenditure, but a section endowed with guaranteed resources seems indispensable nevertheless.

"Owing to the number and variety of cases which may arise, it is important that the States themselves should participate in the operation. The Fund would place certain amounts at their disposal and would make them responsible for working out appropriate solutions in each case, asking them also to provide their own guarantee.

"In addition, this would help to coordinate the reconversion of enterprises and would assist in the re-adaptation of manpower which is foreseen elsewhere: the operations involved would frequently be part of an overall plan. Co-ordination should also be ensured by the work of the European Commission.

"Once the Investment Fund has worked out its interest rate policy, the cost of reconversion loans will appear automatically; but allowance should also be made for any percentage added by the States themselves in order to defray their administrative costs and their guarantee, or alternatively for any interest rebates they may grant to offset the expenses that would otherwise be incurred in financing these operations via the banks or the capital market."

The Rome Treaty

When the Rome Treaty was finally drafted, Article 130 stated the types of projects that the European Investment Bank would finance. At the request of the Italians, who were to be the main recipients of the Bank's loans, less developed regions were placed first on the list. Otherwise, the philosophy of the Spaak Report was adopted in the Treaty:

The task of the European Investment Bank shall be to contribute, by having recourse to the capital market and utilizing its own resources, to the balanced and stable development of the Common Market in the interest of the Community. For this purpose the Bank shall, by granting loans and guarantees on a non-profit-making basis, facilitate the financing of the following projects in all sectors of the economy: (a) projects for developing less developed regions;

(b) projects for modernizing or converting undertakings or for developing fresh activities called for by the progressive establishment of the Common Market where such projects by their size or nature cannot be entirely financed by the various means available in each of the Member States;

(c) projects of common interest to several Member States which by their size or nature cannot be entirely financed by the various means available in the individual Member States.

The capital of the Bank was fixed at 1000 million dollars, of which 25 percent was paid in (France and Germany subscribed 300 million each, Italy 240 million, Belgium 86.5 million, the Netherlands 71.5 million, and Luxembourg 2 million). In addition, the member states undertook to grant, in certain circumstances, special loans to the Bank, with a ceiling of 400 million dollars.

In designating the institution as a bank instead of a fund, the Treaty not only implies greater permanence for it, but also gives it greater financial independence.[9] The way in which the Bank is supposed to operate has been described as follows:

Loans may be granted both to member governments and to public and private enterprises, to the extent that means from other sources are not available on reasonable terms, and subject, as far as possible, to the employment of other means of financing. Loan rates and guarantee commissions must be adapted to conditions prevailing in the capital market and calculated so as to enable the Bank to constitute a reserve fund according to certain rules. There must be no conditions requiring the sums lent by the Bank to be expended within any specific member country. Projects financed by the Bank must meet certain conditions regarding economic utility and financial profitability.

The Bank is supposed to borrow in the international capital markets the funds necessary for its tasks. In the initial stage, however, it is able to devote part of its paid-up capital to lending. A member state may not refuse its consent to the floating of a Bank loan on its capital market unless serious disturbances in that market are to be feared.

The Bank is enjoined to co-operate with the banking and financial institutions of the countries to which it extends its operations. Applica-

[9] The subsequently created European Development Funds (Fund I and Fund II) were designed for African development financing.

tions for loans and guarantees not made by or through the inter-
mediary of the member state concerned must be submitted for an
opinion to that state, and a project must not be financed by the Bank
if it is opposed by the state in whose territory it is to be carried out.

The Bank is administered and managed by a Board of Governors,
a Board of Directors and a Management Committee. The Board of
Governors, composed of the six ministers of finance (or of the treasury
or the budget), lays down the general directives concerning the credit
policy of the Bank, carries the final responsibility for the Bank's operations, and appoints the other two administrative bodies. The Board of
Directors decides on the granting of loans and guarantees and on the
raising of loans, and ensures the sound administration of the Bank. Of
the twelve directors, three each are nominated by France, Germany
and Italy, two by the Benelux countries and one by the European
Commission; they usually act by simple majority vote. The Management Committee, composed of a chairman and two vice-chairmen, is
responsible for the management of the current affairs of the Bank; it
prepares and implements the decisions of the Board of Directors.[10]

Operations of the European Investment Bank

The EIB has not fulfilled the vital role envisioned for it by the
planners of the Rome Treaty. It has plodded along in relatively
low gear, an institution of "cash without clients."[11] This is not to
say that something has gone wrong; on the contrary, the Six, in
general, with the brief exception of Italy in 1963–1964, have not
experienced the balance-of-payments difficulties that were feared
in 1956. As a consequence, the need for the Bank appears to have
been overemphasized by the Spaak Report.

At the end of 1965, the main liabilities of the EIB were as
follows:

Paid-up capital	250 million dollars
Statutory reserves	32
Provision for various contingencies	34
Consolidated debt	217
Total	533

This total excludes the 750 million dollars of unpaid capital.

[10] See Lundstrom, *Capital Movements*, pp. 153–54.
[11] *Common Market* (The Hague), No. 6, June 1962, p. 99.

During its early period of operation, the Bank lent most of its paid-in capital and did not borrow. The total consolidated debt of 217 million dollars was incurred in only five years (1961–1965): seventeen issues were sold, in amounts ranging from 1 to 24 million dollars. The lowest rate of interest was 4½ percent, and the highest 6½ percent. Currencies borrowed were dollars, Swiss francs, and all those of the Six. Total borrowings by the Bank in 1966 were over 100 million dollars.

At the end of 1965, the net amount lent by the EIB (18 million dollars in reimbursements is deducted) was 488 million dollars, of which 366 million had actually been disbursed. The total number of lending operations was 106. One third of these involved loans of less than 1 million dollars, and the average loan was for 5.3 million dollars. These amounts appear rather small; however, their importance is more accurately indicated by taking account of the fact that on the average the Bank intervened only to the extent of 22 percent of the total cost of the projects financed. In 1965 alone, the Bank lent 151 million dollars for 32 projects. The Bank has never acted as a guarantor.

As discussed earlier, the Spaak Report and Article 130 of the Rome Treaty were concerned with directing the loan activities of the EIB. In 1958, the Bank's Board of Governors issued a loan policy directive that provided additional nuances to the order of priorities:

(a) The Bank shall devote a large part of its resources to the financing of projects designed to *improve less developed regions* of the members.

(b) The Bank shall finance projects of *common interest to the members*, particularly projects which are likely to assist in the coordination of markets and the integration of the economies of its members.

(c) In addition to the *financial and economic* standards set forth in the Rome Treaty and the Statute, the Bank shall observe the following principles:

    (i) The Bank shall finance projects of *sufficient* size to avoid widespread dispersal of its resources.

    (ii) Loans made by the Bank shall only *supplement* the resources otherwise available to borrowers for their projects.

    (iii) The Bank shall give *special attention to projects* in which *capital from several member States is invested.*

As implied by their omission from the loan policy directive, loans for reconversion (e.g., shipyards) have been very few. Under Article 130 of the Rome Treaty, assistance for this purpose by the Bank was tied to a requirement that the reconversion be necessary as a consequence of the integration of the Six. The Bank decided that such determination was too difficult and omitted reconversion from its priorities. The Commission has asked the EIB to place more emphasis on reconversion loans in the future.[12]

In line with the order of priorities, nearly all the Bank's loans have been for development purposes. Roughly two thirds have been for innovation, and the other third has been for modernization.

A breakdown by economic sector of the amounts lent through 1965 shows the following:

Agricultural improvements	12 percent
Transport	25
Power	21
Telecommunications	3
Coal mining and steel	8
Other industries	31

Loans to mining and steel enterprises are discussed with the High Authority's civil servants, but there is no formal consultative procedure.

Among the member countries, Italy has been the main beneficiary, receiving 74 loans, or 75 percent of the total amount granted by the Bank. France received 13 loans, Germany 6, Belgium and Luxembourg 1 each, and the Netherlands none. (In addition, Greece, Turkey, and various African countries were granted 20 loans.) This biased distribution is due to the fact that Italy and France have regional development problems, Italy in the

[12] *Europe,* July 10, 1964.

Mezzogiorno and France, to a small extent, in the Southwest, Brittany, and Normandy.

Another factor affecting the loan distribution is the rates of interest asked by the Bank from the borrowers. For instance, on December 20, 1965, these rates were as follows: 6½ percent, up to 7 years; 6½ percent, from 7 to 12 years; 6¾ percent, from 12 to 20 years. One reason no loans have been made in the Netherlands is that Dutch borrowers of good standing could obtain local capital at lower rates than those offered by the EIB.

The Bank's concentration on Italy and, to a lesser extent, on France is also evident in the ratio of EIB loans to total national investment in each of the Six during the 1962–1964 period: between 0.68 and 0.82 percent in Italy, 0.02 and 0.11 percent in France, 0.00 and 0.02 percent in Germany, and nil in the Benelux countries.

The Bank has an exchange guarantee clause because its resources are constituted by a variety of currencies and it may lend in the borrower's own currency. There are in fact two exchange clauses:

(i) Under the first, the Bank lends in a variety of currencies, except in the national currency of the borrowing country. In this instance, the debtor has to repay in the currencies received. Repayment must take place in the monetary equivalent of the amount borrowed, even if there was a change in par values.

(ii) The second alternative provides for lending in one or several currencies, including the borrower's national currency with the debtor repaying in the currency chosen by the Bank. In this case, the par value of the currency on the date of payment is used as the criterion for calculating the cost of repayment, but the Bank cannot require repayment in a currency other than that of a member State. This second alternative provides, *de facto* and *de jure*, for an exchange guarantee. Consequently, interest rates for loans guaranteed under this second alternative are lower than those granted under the first alternative where repayment involves no such guarantee.[13]

[13] Henry S. Bloch, *Regional Development Financing* (United Nations Conference on Trade and Development, Document TD/B/AC4/R3, February 9, 1966, prepared in collaboration with the UN Fiscal and Financial Branch).

Hopes that the EIB would become the nucleus of an active European banking system have been quashed. Private bankers complain that it does not attempt to connect itself with the financial markets and that it is run much more like an administrative agency than a business enterprise.

A description and analysis of the Common Market's financial activities for African development, through both the EIB and the European Development Fund, can be found in *Regional Development Financing*, a report published by the UN in 1966 (see footnote 13).

C: COMMON MARKET FINANCIAL BODIES

In addition to the Monetary Committee, already mentioned several times, a number of other bodies have been established by the Commission or by the Council to function in the area of finance.

The Short-Term Economic Policy Committee was organized in 1960, and two more bodies were established in 1964: the Committee of Governors of Central Banks and the Budget Policy Committee. In all, excluding "gentlemen's agreements" and "informal" meetings between representatives of member states, there are now six committees looking after short-term economic objectives (mainly price stability) and the instruments for their realization. One cannot help feeling that this is too much of a good thing. One or two committees should be disbanded, and a hierarchy of committees should be established to avoid overlapping and repetition.

If new committees continue to sprout, a modern Tower of Babel may result. Already, in the Commission's annual reports, there are successive headings such as "economic and financial policy" and "monetary and financial policy." One of the causes of this confusion is the use of the word "policy" in too many senses. It is applied in EEC documents to all of the following:

Objectives (e.g., competition or regional protection).

Instruments (e.g., money and finance or "commercial policy").

Branches of activity (e.g., agriculture, transport, or energy).

Parts of the administrative framework (e.g., "social policy," which in practice means everything affecting manual workers).

As to the activities of the various short-term policy bodies, the latest initiative of the Commission is directed toward permanent and compulsory consultation with them each time that the economic indicators reach certain levels.[14] The national governments would retain the final say, but they would not be able to act before hearing the views of their partners and of the Commission.

In 1964, overcoming German doubts, the Commission obtained the Council's permission to establish the Medium-Term Economic Policy Committee. The Committee's purpose is to study the trends in national policies, pick out the problems that may result from them at the Community level, and propose to Community institutions the course that it considers will best serve the aims of the Rome Treaty.

The Committee is composed of two members and two alternates from each of the Common Market countries, selected from among senior national officials responsible for general economic policy, together with two members and two alternates representing the Commission. The Committee, in its turn, has set up working parties on structural policy, on incomes policy, and on scientific and technical research policy, as well as a group of experts that prepares comprehensive medium-term economic projections to guide economic policy decisions. At the beginning of 1966 this group handed in its first comprehensive report (for the period 1966–1970), which included forecasts of relative price movements.

In February 1967 the Council adopted the Committee's medium-term economic policy program. This program sets guidelines until 1970 for approaching economic objectives and provides a basis for closer coordination of national policies directed toward these goals. The Commission makes an annual review of the program to

[14] *Europe*, June 22, 1966.

see whether the governments are following the guidelines and to adjust the program in the light of new developments.

Every self-respecting international institution has its own statistical and economic units, which are engaged in economic analysis. This is true, for instance, of the UN, its regional commissions, FAO, IBRD, and OECD. The EEC Commission is no exception; its staff and committees are leading the field with monthly business surveys (in which all countries, except the Netherlands, participate); surveys of investments and investment projects; consumer surveys; yearly economic budgets prepared by the national governments; and, more generally, frequently produced comparative short-term economic statistics, for example, on national accounts.

D: EXPENDITURES AND REVENUES
OF THE EEC COMMISSION

The Commission's expenditures for the period 1961–1966 appear in Table 19. During these five years, administrative expenses doubled, which is more than might have been expected from a combination of price rises in Belgium (15 percent) and the application of Parkinson's law. However, about 60 percent of administrative costs are attributable to the salaries of the Commission's civil servants, and since the Commission's duties have become more and more exacting, a larger and more skilled staff was needed. By any standards the authorized administrative expenditures in 1966 of 42 million dollars are tiny in relation to the Commission's functions; Europe definitely gets good value for what amounts to 0.015 percent of the combined national product of the Six.

The extremely small disbursement figure for the European Social Fund fluctuates around 10 million dollars. For social purposes, the Community spends only about 5 cents per inhabitant (of course, this does not take into account payments by national, state, or local governments).

A look at the agricultural figures tells a very different story. Because of various political and administrative lags, nothing was spent until 1965, although agricultural commitments had begun in 1962. In 1965, however, the authorized agricultural expenditures of 103 million dollars were about double all other expenditures by the Commission; in 1966 the amount was trebled to about 300 million dollars, thus dwarfing administrative and Social Fund expenditures.

Agricultural expenditures are channeled through the European

TABLE 19

EEC Commission Expenditure Authorized and Disbursed[a]
(millions of dollars)

	1961	1962	1963	1964	1965	1966
Wages and salaries	14.1	16.4	19.3	21.3	23.3	26.1
Current purchases of goods and services	6.9	10.4	12.2	12.3	12.0	15.6
1. Total administrative expenditure	21.0	26.8	31.5	33.6	35.3	41.7
	(19.5)	(23.3)	(26.5)	(30.8)	(34.5)	
2. European Social Fund	20.0	29.0	17.8	23.2	19.7	21.6
	(0)	(12.3)	(7.6)	(4.6)	(7.2)	
3. Agricultural guarantee	—	—	—	—	77.0	225.5
					(28.7)	
Orientation (Guidance)	—	—	—	—	25.7	75.2
					(0)	
Total	—	—	—	—	102.7	300.7
					(28.7)	
Grand total	41.1	55.8	49.3	56.8	157.7	364.0
	(19.5)	(35.6)	(34.1)	(35.4)	(70.4)	

Source: *Rapport de la Commission de contrôle de la CEE.*
[a] Amounts actually disbursed are shown in brackets.

Fund for Agricultural Guarantee and Guidance (FEOGA). Three quarters of the money goes to the "guarantee" section, increasing the prices of agricultural products. The remaining quarter is spent by the "guidance" section on structural improvements of agricultural production.

Now that future agricultural prices have been settled between the governments of the Six, it is possible to estimate future expenditures by the FEOGA. By 1970, they should be on the order of 1300 million dollars.[15] Total expenditures by the Commission, including administration and the Social Fund, will reach 1400 million dollars (at 1965 prices). This is equivalent to only 0.37 percent of the present total gross product of the Six and 3 percent of their government expenditures. Nevertheless, at these orders of magnitude, the bitter controversy that arose over the manner in which these future expenditures of the Commission would be financed is understandable.

As discussed earlier in this chapter, the High Authority of the ECSC has the power to tax enterprises under its jurisdiction. This example of an independent revenue source was not followed by the authors of the Rome Treaty. According to Article 200, the Commission's budget revenue shall include, in addition to other revenue, financial contributions from member states, calculated as follows:[16]

Germany, France, and Italy	each 28 percent of the total
Belgium and the Netherlands	each 7.9 percent of the total
Luxembourg	0.2 percent of the total

This system leaves the income of the Commission entirely in the hands of the national governments, apart from "other revenue," which in 1966 accounted for 0.5 percent of the total; most of this came from taxes levied on the salaries of the Commission's civil servants.

[15] "Finance and the Future of the Community," *Common Market* (The Hague), Vol. 5, No. 6 (June 1965).
[16] The scale is slightly different for the expenses of the Social Fund.

With the development of agricultural expenditures, national contributions to the Commission's budget began to increase quickly in 1965, and several studies appeared that attempted to calculate the extent to which some countries benefited more from the FEOGA than they contributed to it. The conclusions of one of the most respected studies are given in Table 20; they show France as the biggest winner and Germany as the main loser. As a consequence, many people have begun to wonder whether the contributions of member states to the Commission's budget should not, to some extent, be altered to compensate for the financial inequalities of the agricultural provisions.

TABLE 20

*Estimated Budgetary Gains and Losses Arising in 1970
from the Activities of the FEOGA
(millions of dollars)*

France	+154.5
Italy	+108
Netherlands	+ 17
Belgium–Luxembourg	− 14
Germany	−265.6

Source: *Common Market*, Vol. 6, No. 6 (June 1966), p. 115.

Another problem arose in 1968, when the Common Market was completed. At that time, importers of non-EEC goods became able to pay the common tariff duties at any point of entry into the Community. Unless preventive steps are taken, this is bound to divert into the coffers of the countries with good harbor facilities (i.e., the Netherlands and Belgium) the proceeds of duties on many goods destined for other Community countries (mainly Germany).

Two solutions can be imagined to this problem: either the countries agree to share customs duties in given proportions (this system works between Belgium and Luxembourg), or the duties could be spent for Community purposes. The latter solution is foreseen in Article 201 of the Rome Treaty, which reads:

The Commission shall study the conditions under which the financial contributions of Member States provided for in Article 200 may be replaced by other resources available to the Community itself, in particular by revenue accruing from the common tariff when finally introduced.

The Commission shall for this purpose submit proposals to the Council.

The Council may, after consulting the Assembly as to these proposals, unanimously determine the provisions which it shall recommend the Member States to adopt in accordance with their respective constitutional requirements.

In March 1965, the Commission thought it could kill two birds with one stone by deciding that the time had come to apply Article 201. Both financial independence from national governments and a tempering of the inequalities resulting from agricultural contributions could be achieved.[17] Explaining the plan, the Commission predicted, for 1972, 1700 million dollars of expenditures and 2400 million dollars of income from customs duties.[18] The balance of some 700 million dollars would be returned by the Commission to the member states, according to economic policy requirements "taking account of the economic and social situation in the various regions of the Community and of the necessity to ensure an equitable distribution of the burdens in the Community." This deliberately vague phrasing in the Commission's proposal would have given the Commission not only financial independence, but also financial influence on the national governments.

For this reason, and also because of the fact that the Commission's proposals would considerably increase the power of the European Parliament (see below), the French Government objected violently:

It rejects the idea of pouring the proceeds of industrial tariffs into EEC coffers and proposes the following solution to the problem of the dis-

---

[17] See *Europe*, April 8 and 10, 1965.

[18] "Commission Proposal for EEC Budget Heralds Growing Economic Sovereignty for Community," *Business Europe* (Geneva), March 24, 1965.

tortion of customs proceeds in favor of those member states with better port facilities: government-to-government redistribution of a proportion of the industrial duties to countries of final import destination.

The member countries, say the French, should also collect their own duties on agricultural imports from third countries, then pass them on to the Commission for the financing of EEC farm surplus exports, modernization of agriculture and support of farm prices. The Commission should have no say in commercial agreements with third countries that call for FEOGA-subsidized agricultural exports, but leave each country fully sovereign—until political union *à la francaise* renders possible the harmonization of external trade policies.[19]

At the end of June 1965, the French withdrew their delegates from most of the Community's institutions. They finally resumed co-operation in May 1966. The compromise, reached after months of painful negotiation, provides as follows:

The smooth functioning of the EEC farm policy, whose main target is the improvement of farmer's incomes through high common prices for major commodities, rests on the two-pronged FEOGA.

Acting as a clearing bank and a supranational quasi-treasury, FEOGA essentially is: (1) the final recipient of all levies (90 percent until 1970) collected by member states on third-country farm imports (levies are in effect equal to the difference between the world market price and a fictitious EEC price); (2) the disbursing agency for subsidies to member states that export farm surpluses not marketable in the EEC; and (3) the regulator of internal farm-product markets. Up to 1970, the levies will account for about 45 percent of FEOGA's "guarantee" expenses while the balance will be supplied by exchequer contributions from the member states, according to a fixed scale for each country (with the French Government contributing the larger portion).

Under its aids-to-agriculture "orientation" program, FEOGA will apportion a maximum of $285 million annually among member states for improving agricultural life. But here the member states themselves will entirely foot the bill (until 1970) in the form of direct budget grants, again according to a fixed scale. After 1970, the resources needed by FEOGA to cover both its "guarantee" and its "orientation"

[19] "Common Market's Bickering Ministers Bury Community Budget but Bolster Kennedy Round," *Business Europe* (Geneva), May 19, 1965.

expenses will come solely from the supranational Community's own resources (i.e., 100% of levies and certainly also import duties on third-country industrial products).[20]

A decision on the disposition of the proceeds from the common external tariff has been postponed; meanwhile, care will be taken to discourage distortions in favor of the countries enjoying the best port facilities.

Expenditures by national governments are generally submitted to administrative and to parliamentary supervision. The authors of the Rome Treaty thought that the Common Market institutions should be subject to the same scrutiny. Consequently, the Rome Treaty provides that the Commission shall present each year to the Council a draft proposal consolidating estimated expenditures for all the Community institutions in the coming year. On the basis of this proposal, the Council prepares a draft budget that it must present to the Assembly for comments and suggestions for amendment. This administrative supervision seems to have worked smoothly,[21] despite the fact that the Assembly has only a consultative role, at the insistence of the French negotiators of the Treaty.

When the Commission submitted to the Council its ill-fated financial proposals of March 1965, it suggested that the European Parliament—presumably elected directly by the people—be given the right to modify the draft budgets submitted to it. The Council could then modify these proposals by a simple majority vote if it agreed with the Commission, or otherwise by a vote of five to one. This would have meant that no one government would have been able to veto budgetary proposals in the Council:[22] controlling the

[20] "How FEOGA Will Function," *Business Europe* (Geneva), May 18, 1966.

[21] See M. Bauchard, "Les budgets des institutions Européennes de Bruxelles et le contrôle de leur exécution," Conférence du 23 janvier 1963 à l'Institut des Sciences Politiques de Paris.

[22] A qualified majority vote of the Council is all that the Treaty presently requires for the Council to adopt a budget; however, the Ministers have always required unanimity among themselves.

spending of European money would become a matter of main concern in the European Parliament, not just in the national parliaments.

Five governments were ready to accept this important transfer of power, but despite France's enormous benefits from the common agricultural expenditures, the French Government, for political reasons, refused to budge.[23] De Gaulle could not accept a procedure whereby issues vital to France could be settled by a majority of "aliens."

The compromise agreements of May 1966 left the matter in abeyance. It is impossible to predict whether anything will happen in this field before the end of 1970.

E: EUROPEAN COMPANIES

Origin

The greater inter-European competition resulting from the integration process will lead to problems of survival for enterprises that are not strong enough to adapt themselves to the new market conditions. In fact, most undertakings will be obliged to develop their organization, increase their capital, intensify their research, and perhaps associate with other companies. Concentrations to increase productive capacity are desirable because they stimulate competitive strength among business groups.

According to each nation's legislation, companies may participate in concentrations taking place within the member states, but legal obstacles prevent a merger between enterprises from different countries. To overcome these difficulties and help clear the way toward full economic union, the introduction of a European company has been considered by a number of authors. This solution would prevent the governments of the Six from adopting company

---

[23] J. Doumont, "Le débat agricole des Six; ses conséquences économiques, financières, politiques," *Cahiers économiques de Bruxelles*, No. 27, 1965.

laws even more in conflict with each other than those presently in force.

The idea of some kind of European company statute has been in the air since the beginning of the Common Market.[24] In 1960, an international congress, organized by the Bar of the Paris Court, brought together legal experts and business representatives to discuss the difficulties encountered in international relations because of disparities in corporation laws. The desirability of creating a company governed by a system of European law was examined with conclusive affirmative results.[25]

The French Proposal

In March 1965, the French Government proposed the creation of a European company enjoying equal legal status throughout the Common Market. According to the French proposal, uniform legislation would be enacted by each country individually, with each company free to opt for either the present national charter or for the new uniform European charter.

The main consideration behind France's proposal was that the uniform European company formula would facilitate cross-border industrial concentration, as well as rationalization through joint manufacturing subsidiaries or research and development centers, and would pave the way for full-fledged mergers when harmonization of direct taxes makes them possible, that is, not before 1970. The organizational structure of the uniform European company would also

- help large companies to exercise stricter control over their network of EEC subsidiaries, which would be subject to the same laws;
- encourage private investors to put capital into industrial

[24] L. Larcier, "Le placement mobilier dans le Marché Commun," *La Revue de la Banque* (Brussels), No. 2, 1959, p. 139.

[25] "Congrès international pour la création d'une société commerciale de type Européen," *Compte rendu des travaux*, June 16, 17, 18, 1960 (supplement to *Revue du Marché Commun*, No. 27, July–August 1960).

groups offering the same legal guarantees in the whole Community regardless of their incorporation site;

- encourage small firms to set up subsidiaries in countries whose legislation would no longer be unfamiliar to them;
- facilitate transfer of corporate headquarters from one EEC country to another without changing the by-laws;
- favor intra-EEC trade by placating consumers' resistance to products made in foreign countries.

The company's name, which would be the same in all member countries, should be legally protected in each member state. The company should have a minimum capital and a minimum number of stockholders. Certain privileges could be established for founders and initial shareholders. When incorporating a uniform EEC company, firms could choose either to submit their by-laws for official registration or to establish them under authenticated deeds. The need to protect minority shareholders and creditors should not infringe upon management's freedom of action. Decision-making powers should be entrusted to a supervisory council or a board of directors, depending on whether or not the Company issued shares to the public. Shareholders should be well informed of the company's operations, and a minority should be free to relinquish its interest if the company renounced its European status or substantially transferred its activities. Presentation and verification of accounts should be uniform. The uniform European company would be subject to the national jurisdiction of the country of incorporation, but to preserve its uniform multinational character, national jurisprudence would have to be harmonized as regards interpretation of the uniform company law.[26]

There is one basic weakness in the French proposal for a uniform company law. This form of unified legislation does not

---

[26] See J. Foyer, "La proposition française de création d'une société de type Européen," *Revue du Marché Commun*, No. 81, June 1965; and "France Proposes 'European Company,'" *Business Europe* (Geneva), April 7, 1965.

prevent the changes of corporate nationality that occur when a company transfers its seat of incorporation from one jurisdiction to another. This is one of the main impediments to uniform company laws because national governments are worried about losing their jurisdictional base for purposes of taxation.

The Commission's Proposal

The Commission has recently examined the possibility of going beyond the French proposal by creating a new type of company charter giving corporations legal rights throughout the Common Market.[27] The Commission published a memorandum proposing the introduction of a supranational company whose juridical existence would be based upon a transnational enabling statute, which would take effect when a convention enacting the common EEC legislation is ratified by each member state. Rights of interpretation would be assigned to the European Court of Justice in Luxembourg, serving as a court of last resort.[28]

The introduction of a European corporation law would offer all the advantages mentioned in connection with the French proposal, plus several additional ones that are available only under a supranational plan. At the same time, because it is much more ambitious, the Commission's plan raises more problems. Therefore, after proposing what appears to be the most effective formula for creating a European company law, the Commission's memorandum goes on to outline the other obstacles to industrial concentration and competition that must still be ironed out. For instance, even though the enactment of a European company law would spare managers the problems entailed by the selection of the final nationality in cross-border mergers, capital gains arising from such operations

[27] Commission, "*Mémorandum de la Commission de la Communauté économique Européenne sur la création d'une société commerciale Européenne,*" CEE (SEC/66 1250 22.4, 1966).
[28] See "EEC Integrationists Score in Brussels: Commission to Recommend Supranational Company Law," *Business Europe* (Geneva), April 27, 1966.

could still be taxed differently by each member state. Also, while a European company law would undoubtedly stimulate capital movements across national frontiers by facilitating private investments in companies offering equal guarantees throughout the Common Market, national regulations could prevent EEC firms from freely issuing their shares in any of the national capital markets.

In short, the establishment of companies under European law depends on a coherent solution of a vast number of other legal problems in the areas of fiscal, financial, social, and corporate regulation. Before making a definite choice between the establishment of European companies under a system of uniform national laws and establishment under a European law, the Commission must know the results of detailed expert investigations already under way.

The Commission and the French Government have agreed to create a working party of national and Community experts to investigate the problems that would accompany the different proposals. High on the list of topics to be studied by the panel will be the harmonization of direct corporate income taxes.

F: MONEY

The Present Situation

European financial integration will not be complete until there is a uniform currency among the Six. Achieving this will be difficult because, although money is no longer the kingpin of economic policy, it has remained very important to the man in the street. It is the symbol of national prestige, the economic equivalent of the national anthem and the national flag. As a consequence, for purely political reasons, the early prospects for a uniform currency appear slim, barring an unexpected upheaval of some sort in international monetary matters.

Exchange rates between the currencies of the Six have a good chance of remaining fixed. If there is alteration, it will come only after lengthy consultations have produced a clear view of all the consequences. Unilateral decisions in this area are a thing of the past. Nowadays, ministers of finance, governors of central banks, and their technical advisers meet regularly in a European forum and are quite familiar with each other's objectives, instruments, and problems. The mutual assistance arranged by Article 108 of the Rome Treaty for member states in balance-of-payments difficulties has been applied only once, after France experienced a general strike during the summer of 1968. Therefore, although a dialogue has been established and interdependence recognized, further willingness to sacrifice personal, institutional, and national financial power on the altar of European integration has hardly been tested.

We shall now analyze three possibilities for further progress toward monetary integration: a monetary union, a partial pooling of exchange reserves, and a Common Market central bank. These three, in the order given, entail increasing sacrifices of national power and thus decreasing probabilities of realization in the near future. Since a partial pooling of exchange reserves is the most interesting integration strategy, we will discuss it in more detail than the other two approaches.

This proposal will not be fulfilled before the end of the transitional period. In fact, the "federal type banking system" is so far in the future that only mention of the fact that it has been proposed is justified. The monetary adjustment problems characterizing the 1960s are strongly aggravated by the absence of a European Central Bank. As such a federal banking system is not yet in sight, these adjustment troubles will not fail to reoccur in the years ahead.

A Monetary Union

In the nineteenth century, France, Belgium, Switzerland, Italy, and Greece entered into what was called "l'union latine." Their gold and silver coins were interchangeable at par and, in the case of the first three countries, bore the same names. With this historical antecedent, it is possible to imagine the Six establishing a similar monetary union, whereby they would have six currencies called francs—if the Germans, Italians, and Dutch consented—or gold ducats, a respectable old name that has been suggested.[29] The "unit of account," mentioned in many international conventions, is too clumsy, and the "Eurodollar" would not appeal to European nationalism, apart from other defects.[30] Whatever its name, the setting up of a European currency unit would require overcoming Dutch and German opposition, demonstrated by the refusal of these countries to allow such a move by the European Investment Bank in its borrowing operations. [31]

A monetary union implying automatic and unlimited credit from one central bank to another has been suggested;[32] however, this will not be feasible for many years. In the meantime, the type of monetary union envisioned is almost purely a propaganda gimmick; at most, it is a very modest step toward harmonization. However, its importance in promoting monetary integration should not be underestimated; propaganda is often a powerful tool.

A Partial Pooling of Exchange Reserves

The third possibility would be the creation of a European Reserve Fund managed jointly by the Six in their common interest, but with national ministers of finance and central banks retaining most of their functions. This was proposed by Professor

[29] Pictoro Formentini, *Per una moneta commune Europea* (Bancaria, Rome, 1959), pp. 575–77.

[30] See B. J. Cohen, "The Euro-dollar, the Common Market and Currency Unification," *The Journal of Finance*, December 1963.

[31] See P. Kern, "Vers une monnaie unique en Europe?" *Revue du Marché Commun,* July–August 1963, Paris.

[32] A. Day, "Les implications financières du Marché Commun," *Cahiers de l'Institut de Service Economique Appliqué* (Paris, May 1962).

Robert Triffin in 1960[33] and was taken up in 1962 by the Commission in its action program for the second stage:

An intergovernmental agreement should lay down now the extent of the obligations which each country is prepared to accept with regard to mutual aid under the Treaty, without such prior agreement in any way prejudging the question of whether the Member State in difficulty fulfills the conditions under which aid is to be given.

But, if an affirmative decision was given on this latter point, the maximum credits which Member States had committed themselves to make available would be known in advance. These credits should represent a certain proportion of the gold and foreign exchange reserves held by each of the Community Central Banks, so as to take into account changes which might occur in the international liquidity situation of any Member State.[34]

Whereas the Commission contented itself with principles, Triffin proceeded to advocate the proposal in further detail.[35] He suggested that the EEC set up a financial body consisting of the finance ministers and the governors of the central banks to decide, by simple majority rule, overall policy for the administration and investment of a given proportion of the monetary reserves of the central banks. This proportion would initially be 25–30 percent (in 1963, 4.5–5 billion dollars), the equivalent of various credits already granted or promised to the International Monetary Fund and to other central banks in the Group of Ten. The proportion could be progressively increased to 40 or 50 percent by a series of votes requiring a qualified majority. The financial body, the European Reserve Fund, would invest the amounts under its control

---

[33] R. Triffin, *Intégration économique Européenne et politique monétaire. La restauration des monnaies européennes* (Paris, Sirey, 1960). The idea was also approved by the Action Committee for the United States of Europe and by *The Economist* (London): "An Idea for Aid," December 12, 1959.

[34] See Commission, EEC, *Memorandum on the Action Program for the Second Stage*, pp. 63–67.

[35] R. Triffin, "La Communauté économique Européenne et la coopération monétaire internationale," *Les problèmes de l'Europe* (Paris-Rome), No. 19, 1963, pp. 188–200.

either in mutual assistance under Article 108 of the Rome Treaty, in net claims on the International Monetary Fund, in reciprocal support credits under negotiated agreements (swaps and standbys), in direct support loans (classical sterling and dollar balances), or in gold. Such decisions would presumably be taken by a qualified majority vote.

However, six months before the action program for the second stage was released, the Monetary Committee, in anticipation, poured cold water on the Commission's proposal:

The gradual attainment of the various aims which form part of the Common Market will mean that *when the time comes to change over from co-ordination to centralization of decisions*, the transition will *appear to be nothing more than one more* step forward. Quite apart from purely political factors, which are outside the competence of the Committee, technical grounds will prevent this transition being made before the economic and financial structure of the Member States has been made much more homogeneous. Just as the move to convertibility appeared possible only when the situation was ripe on the internal plane in different countries, so too their economic and financial structure will have to undergo many changes before it will in practice be possible to adopt a more centralized policy.[36]

This was tantamount to a rejection of the European Reserve Fund.[37] Subsequently, the Monetary Committee has done nothing to advance the Commission's proposal and neither has the Committee of Finance Ministers or the Committee of Governors of Central Banks. Triffin[38] attributes this negative attitude to the fact that central banks are traditionally jealous of their independence and particularly distrustful of any "expansionist" move likely to open the gate to inflationist abuses. Dieterlen[39] pushes this psychological analysis somewhat further and attributes negativism partly

[36] European Economic Community, *Fourth Report on the Activities of the Monetary Committee* (Brussels, April 15, 1962).

[37] See "The Construction of Monetary Policy," *Common Market* (The Hague), June 1962, p. 97.

[38] Triffin, *Intégration économique Européene et politique monétaire*, p. 79.

[39] P. Dieterlen, "La collaboration monétaire entre les Six" Renforcer la Coopération Economique en Europe Ligue Européenne de Coopération Economique (Brussels, June 1963), p. 106.

to the political motivations of some rulers, but mainly to conservative civil servants, jealous of their national prerogatives and fearful of outside suggestions.

Perhaps these two authors tend to exaggerate the difficulties. Giscard d'Estaing, former French Minister of Finance, declared himself in favor of the creation, before July 1968, of a European Bank: "In the absence of a common money a European Bank would allow the setting up of a common monetary policy; this bank would receive 20% of the exchange reserves at present held by the Central Banks and its action would gradually build up the conditions for the issue of a common money."[40]

It is unlikely that a European Reserve Fund will be created without the prompting of changes in other areas of the Community's environment. For example, a general realignment of the main world currencies could provide the incentive for rapid agreement on the pooling of reserves.

The Fund remains a real possibility, but the generally disturbed international situation of the 1960s has contributed to delaying action. In the 1970s there is an excellent chance to see the emergence of a European Reserve Fund as one of the important steps towards international monetary reform.

A European Central Bank

In its 1962 program of action for the second stage, the Commission planned for complete monetary union:

The establishment of the monetary union could become the objective of the third stage towards the Common Market. The Community Ministers of Finance or of Economics, meeting in the Council, would decide on the conditions to be laid down at the appropriate time: the total volume of the national budgets and of the Community budget, and the general conditions for financing them. The Council of the Governors of the Banks of Issue would become the central organ of a federal type banking system.[41]

[40] *Le Monde,* June 7, 1966.
[41] Commission, European Economic Community, *Memorandum on the Action Program for the Second Stage* (Brussels, October 1962), p. 67.

APPENDIX I

A: THE MAIN INSTITUTIONS

THE COMMISSION

Article 155
In order to ensure that the Common Market works efficiently and
develops satisfactorily, the Commission shall
- ensure that the provisions of this Treaty and the measures taken
  by the institutions by virtue of this Treaty are carried out;
- formulate recommendations or give opinions on matters within
  the scope of this Treaty, if it expressly so provides or if the
  Commission considers this necessary;
- have power itself to take decisions and in the circumstances provided for in this Treaty participate in the shaping of measures
  taken by the Council and by the Assembly;
- exercise the powers conferred on it by the Council to ensure
  effect being given to rules laid down by the latter.

Article 156
The Commission shall publish annually, not later than one month
before the opening of the session of the Assembly, a general report on
the activities of the Community.

Article 157

1. The Commission shall consist of nine members, who shall be chosen on grounds of their general competence and whose independence can be fully guaranteed.

   The Council may by a unanimous decision amend the number of the members of the Commission.

   Only nationals of Member States may be members of the Commission.

   The Commission shall not include more than two members having the nationality of the same State.

2. The members of the Commission shall act completely independently in the performance of their duties, in the general interest of the Community.

   In the performance of their duties, they shall neither seek nor take instructions from any Government or other body. They shall refrain from any action incompatible with the nature of their duties. Each Member State undertakes to respect this principle and not to seek to influence the members of the Commission in the performance of their duties.

   The members of the Commission may not, during their term of office, engage in any other paid or unpaid occupation. When entering upon their duties they shall give a solemn undertaking that, both during and after their term of office, they will respect the obligations arising therefrom and in particular their duty to exercise honesty and discretion as regards the acceptance, after their term of office, of particular appointments or benefits. In the event of any breach of these obligations, the Court of Justice, on the application of the Council or of the Commission, may, according to the circumstances, order that the member concerned either be compulsorily retired in accordance with the provisions of Article 160 or forfeit his right to a pension or other benefits in lieu thereof.

Article 158

The members of the Commission shall be appointed by mutual agreement between the Governments of Member States.

Their term of office shall be for a period of four years. It shall be renewable.

Article 163

The Commission shall reach its conclusions by a majority of the number of members provided for in Article 157.

A meeting of the Commission shall only be valid if the number of members laid down in its rules of procedure are present.

THE COUNCIL

Article 145

To ensure the achievement of the objectives laid down in this Treaty, and in accordance with the provisions thereof, the Council shall:

- ensure that the economic policies of the Member States are co-ordinated;
- have power to take decisions.

The Council shall consist of representatives of the Member States. Each Government shall delegate to it one of its members.

The Office of the President shall be exercised for a term of six months by each member of the Council in rotation following the alphabetical order of the Member States.

Article 147

Meetings of the Council shall be called by the President on his own initiative or at the request of a member or of the Commission.

Article 148

1. Except where otherwise provided for in this Treaty, the Council's resolutions shall be reached by a majority of its members.
2. Where the Council's resolutions are required to be reached by qualified majority, the votes of its members shall be weighted as follows:

Belgium	2	Italy	4
France	4	Luxembourg	1
Germany	4	Netherlands	2

The following majorities shall be required for the adoption of resolutions:

- twelve votes in favor where the Treaty requires them to be taken on a proposal of the Commission;
- twelve votes in favor, cast by at least four members, in all other cases.

3. Abstentions by members either present or represented shall not prevent the adoption by the Council of decisions which require to be unanimous.

Article 149

When, in accordance with this Treaty, the Council acts on a proposal of the Commission, it may only adopt amendments to that proposal unanimously.

The Commission shall be free to amend its original proposal at any time before the Council reaches a decision, especially if the Assembly has been consulted on the proposal in question.

THE ASSEMBLY

Article 137

The Assembly, which shall consist of representatives of the peoples of the States united within the Community, shall exercise the advisory and supervisory powers which are conferred upon it by this Treaty.

Article 138

1. The Assembly shall consist of delegates who shall be nominated by the respective Parliaments from among their members in accordance with the procedure laid down by each Member State.
2. The number of these delegates shall be as follows:

Belgium	14	Italy	36
France	36	Luxembourg	6
Germany	36	Netherlands	14

3. The Assembly shall draw up proposals for elections by direct universal suffrage in accordance with a uniform procedure in all Member States.

    The Council shall unanimously decide on the provisions which it shall recommend to Member States for adoption in accordance with their respective constitutional requirements.

Article 141

Except where otherwise provided for in this Treaty, the Assembly shall act by an absolute majority of the votes cast.

The quorum shall be laid down in the rules of procedure.

Article 143

The Assembly shall discuss in open session the annual general report submitted to it by the Commission.

Article 144

If a vote of censure on the activities of the Commission is tabled in the Assembly, no vote shall be taken thereon until not less than three days after it was tabled and this vote shall be by open ballot.

If the vote of censure is carried by a two-thirds majority of the votes cast, and representing a majority of the members of the Assembly, the members of the Commission shall collectively resign their office. They shall continue to carry out current business until their replacement in accordance with the provisions of Article 158.

THE COURT OF JUSTICE

Article 164

The Court of Justice shall ensure the observance of law in the interpretation and application of this Treaty.

The Court of Justice shall consist of seven judges.

The Court of Justice shall sit in plenary session (*séance plénière*). It may, however, set up sections (*chambres*), each consisting of three or five judges, either to take certain steps of investigation (instruction), or to judge particular categories of cases in accordance with the provisions of a regulation made for this purpose.

The Court of Justice shall, however, always sit in plenary session to hear cases submitted to it by a Member State or by one of the institutions of the Community or to deal with the preliminary questions submitted to it pursuant to Article 177.

Should the Court of Justice so request, the Council may, by a unanimous decision, increase the number of judges, and make the consequential amendments to the second and third paragraphs of this Article and Article 167, second paragraph.

Article 169

If the Commission considers that a Member State has failed to fulfill any of its obligations under this Treaty, it shall issue a reasoned opinion on the matter after giving the State concerned the opportunity to submit its comments.

If the State concerned does not comply with the terms of such opinion within the period laid down by the Commission, the latter may refer the matter to the Court of Justice.

Article 171

If the Court of Justice finds that a Member State has failed to fulfill any of its obligations under this Treaty, such State is bound to take the measures required for the implementation of the judgment of the Court.

Article 182

The Court of Justice shall be competent to decide any dispute between Member States connected with the subject of this Treaty, where the said States submit the said dispute to the Court under a special agreement between them.

Article 187

The judgments of the Court of Justice shall be enforceable.

B: FREE MOVEMENT OF NONAGRICULTURAL GOODS AMONG THE SIX

Article 9

1. The Community shall be based upon a *customs union* which shall cover all trade in goods and which shall include the prohibition as between Member States of customs duties on imports and exports and of all charges having equivalent effect, and the adoption of a common customs tariff as against third countries.

Article 30

Quantitative restrictions on imports and all measures having equivalent effect shall, without prejudice to the following provisions, be prohibited as between Member States.

Article 34

1. *Quantitative restrictions on exports,* and any measures having equivalent effect, are prohibited as between Member States.
2. Member States shall, at latest by the end of the first stage, abolish all quantitative restrictions on exports and any measures having equivalent effect which are in existence when this Treaty comes into force.

Article 13

1. *Customs duties on imports* in force as between Member States shall be gradually abolished by them during the transitional period.
2. Taxes having an equivalent effect to customs duties on imports in force as between Member States shall be gradually abolished by them during the transitional period. The Commission shall determine by means of directives the timetable for such abolition.

Article 14
1. For each product, the basic duty to which the *successive reductions* shall apply shall be the duty applied on January 1, 1957.
2. The timetable for the reductions shall be determined as follows:
   (a) during the first stage, the first reduction shall be made one year after the date when this Treaty comes into force; the second reduction, eighteen months later; and the third reduction, at the end of the fourth year after the date when this Treaty comes into force;
   (b) during the second stage, a reduction shall be made eighteen months after its commencement; a second reduction, eighteen months after the preceding one; and a third reduction, one year later;
   (c) any remaining reductions shall be made during the third stage; the Council shall determine the timetable by means of directives, by a qualified majority vote on a proposal of the Commission.

Article 16
Member States shall, as between themselves, abolish *customs duties on exports* and charges having equivalent effect at latest by the end of the first stage.

C: FREE MOVEMENT OF AGRICULTURAL GOODS
AMONG THE SIX

This is a very complicated matter to which ten articles of the Treaty are devoted; the most important are as follows:

Article 38
1. *The Common Market shall extend to agriculture and trade in agricultural products.* The term "agricultural products" shall mean the products of the soil, of stock-breeding and of fisheries and products which have been subjected to first-stage processing and are directly related to the afore-mentioned products.
2. The rules laid down for the establishment of the Common Market shall apply to agricultural products, except where there are provisions to the contrary.
   . . .

4. The operation and development of the Common Market for agricultural products must be accompanied by the establishment of a common agricultural policy among the Member States.

Article 39
1. *The objectives of the common agricultural policy* shall be:
    (a) to increase agricultural productivity by promoting technical progress and by ensuring the rational development of agricultural production and the optimum utilization of all factors of production, in particular labor;
    (b) thus to ensure a fair standard of living for the agricultural community, particularly by increasing the individual earnings of persons engaged in agriculture;
    (c) to stabilize markets;
    (d) to guarantee supplies;
    (e) to ensure the delivery of supplies to consumers at reasonable prices.
2. In working out the common agricultural policy and any special methods which this may involve, account shall be taken of:
    (a) the distinctive nature of agricultural activity, which results from agriculture's social structure and from structural and natural disparities between the various agricultural regions;
    (b) the need to effect the appropriate adjustments gradually;
    (c) the fact that, in the Member States, agriculture constitutes a sector closely linked with the economy as a whole.

Article 40
1. *Member States shall gradually develop a common agricultural policy* during the transitional period and shall bring it into force not later than at the end of that period.
2. In order to achieve the objectives set out in Article 39 a common organization for agricultural markets shall be established.
    This organization shall take one of the following forms depending on the product concerned:
    (a) common rules as regards competition;
    (b) compulsory coordination of the various national marketing organizations; or
    (c) a European marketing organization.
3. The common organization established in accordance with paragraph 2 of this Article may include all measures required to

achieve the objectives set out in Article 39, in particular price controls, subsidies for the production and distribution of the various products, arrangements for stock-piling and carry-forward, and common arrangements for the stabilization of imports and exports.

The common organization shall confine itself to pursuing the objectives set out in Article 39 and shall exercise no discrimination between producers or consumers within the Community.

Any common price policy shall be based on common criteria and uniform methods of calculation.

4. In order to enable the common organization referred to in paragraph 2 of this Article to achieve its objectives, one or more agricultural orientation and guarantee funds may be set up.

D: FREEDOM OF ESTABLISHMENT AND FREEDOM TO SUPPLY SERVICES

Article 52

Within the framework of the provisions set out below, *restrictions on the freedom of establishment* of nationals of a Member State in the territory of another Member State shall be abolished by progressive stages in the course of the transitional period. Such progressive abolition shall also apply to restrictions on the setting up of agencies, branches or subsidiaries by nationals of any Member State established in the territory of any Member State.

Freedom of establishment shall include the right to engage in and carry on non-wage-earning activities, to set up and manage undertakings.

Article 59

With the framework of the provisions set out below, *restrictions on the freedom of provision of services* within the Community shall be progressively abolished during the transitional period in respect of nationals of Member States who are established in a State of the Community other than that of the person for whom the services are intended.

The Council, acting unanimously, on a proposal of the Commission, may extend the provisions of this Chapter to include services provided by nationals of a third country who are established within the Community.

Article 60

Services within the meaning of this Treaty shall be deemed to be services normally provided against remuneration, in so far as they are not governed by the provisions relating to the free movement of goods, capital and persons.

Services shall include in particular:

(a) activities of an industrial character;

(b) activities of a commercial character;

(c) artisan activities;

(d) activities of the liberal professions.

Without prejudice to the provisions of the Chapter relating to the right of establishment, the person providing a service may in order to carry out that service temporarily practice his activity in the State where the service is provided, under the same conditions as are imposed by that State on its own nationals.

E: FREE MOVEMENT OF WORKERS

Article 48

1. The free movement of labor shall be secured within the Community not later than by the end of the transitional period.

2. Such freedom of movement shall entail the abolition of any discrimination based on nationality between workers of the Member States as regards employment, remuneration and other labor conditions.

3. It shall entail the right, subject to limitations justified on the grounds of public policy (*ordre public*), public security and public health:

   (a) to accept offers of employment actually made;

   (b) to move freely within the territory of Member States for this purpose;

   (c) to stay in a Member State for the purpose of employment in accordance with the legislative and administrative regulations governing the employment of nationals of that state;

   (d) to remain in the territory of a Member State after having been employed in that State, subject to conditions which shall be the subject of implementing regulations to be drawn up by the Commission.

4. The provisions of this Article shall not apply to employment in the public service.

Article 85

1. The following practices shall be prohibited as incompatible with the Common Market: all agreements between undertakings, all decisions by associations of undertakings and all concerted practices which are liable to affect trade between Member States and which are designed to prevent, restrict or distort competition within the Common Market or which have this effect. This shall, in particular, include:

   (a) the direct or indirect fixing of purchase or selling prices or of any other trading conditions;
   (b) the limitation or control of production, markets, technical development or investment;
   (c) market-sharing or the sharing of sources of supply;
   (d) the application of unequal conditions to parties undertaking equivalent engagements in commercial transactions, thereby placing them at a competitive disadvantage;
   (e) making the conclusion of a contract subject to the acceptance by the other party to the contract of additional obligations, which, by their nature or according to commercial practice have no connection with the subject of such contract.

2. Any agreements or decisions prohibited pursuant to this Article shall automatically be null and void.

3. The provisions of paragraph 1 may, however, be declared inapplicable in the case of

   - any agreement or type of agreement between undertakings,
   - any decision or type of decision by associations of undertakings, and
   - any concerted practice or type of concerted practice

   which helps to improve the production or distribution of goods or to promote technical or economic progress, whilst allowing consumers a fair share of the resulting profit and which does not:

   (a) subject the concerns in question to any restrictions which are not indispensable to the achievement of the above objectives;
   (b) enable such concerns to eliminate competition in respect to a substantial part of the goods concerned.

Article 86

Any improper exploitation by one or more undertakings of a dominant position within the Common Market or within a substantial part of it shall be deemed to be incompatible with the Common Market and shall be prohibited, in so far as trade between Member States could be affected by it. The following practices, in particular, shall be deemed to amount to improper exploitation:

(a) the direct or indirect imposition of any unfair purchase or selling prices or of any other unfair trading conditions;

(b) the limitation of production, markets or technical development to the prejudice of consumers;

(c) the application of unequal conditions to parties undertaking equivalent engagements in commercial transactions, thereby placing them at a commercial disadvantage;

(d) making the conclusion of a contract subject to the acceptance by the other party to the contract of additional obligations which their nature or according to commercial practice have no connection with the subject of such contract.

APPENDIX II

LIBERALIZATION OF CAPITAL FLOWS

BEFORE THE ROME TREATY

1. The first attempt at liberalizing international capital flows was that of the International Monetary Fund. Its statutes, agreed to in 1944, provide in Article 14 for the removal of exchange restrictions by member countries.

Section 2. Exchange restrictions

In the postwar transitional period members may, notwithstanding the provisions of any other articles of this Agreement, maintain and adapt to changing circumstances (and, in the case of members whose territories have been occupied by the enemy, introduce where necessary) restrictions on payments and transfers for current international transactions. Members shall, however, have continuous regard in their foreign exchange policies to the purposes of the Fund; and, as soon as conditions permit, they shall take all possible measures to develop such commercial and financial arrangements with other members as will facilitate international payments and the maintenance of exchange stability. In particular, members shall withdraw restrictions maintained or imposed under this Section as soon as they are satisfied that they will be able, in the absence of such restrictions, to settle their balance of payments in a manner which will not unduly encumber their access to the resources of the Fund.

The Fund must also take various actions:

Section 4. Action of the Fund relating to restrictions

Not later than three years after the date on which the Fund begins operations and in each year thereafter, the Fund shall report on the restrictions still in force under Section 2 of this Article. Five years after the date on which the Fund begins operations, and in each year thereafter, any member still retaining any restrictions inconsistent with Article VIII, Section 2, 3 or 4, shall consult the Fund as to their further retention. The Fund may, if it deems such action necessary in exceptional circumstances, make representations to any members that conditions are: favorable for the withdrawal of any particular restriction, or for the general abandonment of restrictions, inconsistent with the provisions of any other article of this Agreement. The member shall be given a suitable time to reply to such representations. If the Fund finds that the member persists in maintaining restrictions which are inconsistent with the purposes of the Fund, the member shall be subject to Article 15, Section 2(a).

A yearly report produced by the Fund contains information, presented in a rather technical way, on restrictions to capital movement kept by the Six.

2. The OECD code contains a number of undertakings binding its 22 members (including all EEC countries). Its Article 1 reads as follows:

(a) Members shall progressively abolish between one another, in accordance with the provisions of Article 2, restrictions on movements of capital to the extent necessary for effective economic cooperation. Measures designed to eliminate such restrictions are hereinafter called "measures of liberalization."
(b) Members shall, in particular, endeavor:
   (i) to treat all non-resident-owned assets in the same way irrespective of the date of their formation, and
   (ii) to permit the liquidation of all non-resident-owned assets and the transfer of such assets or of their liquidation proceeds.
(c) Members should use their best offices to ensure that the measures of liberalization are applied within their overseas territories.
(d) Members shall endeavor to extend the measures of liberalization to all members of the International Monetary Fund.
(e) Members shall endeavor to avoid introducing any new exchange restrictions on the movement of capital or the use of non-resident-owned funds and shall endeavor to avoid making existing regulations more restrictive.

3. The Benelux Treaty, linking three of the EEC countries

(Belgium, the Netherlands, and Luxembourg) in an economic union has provided since June 1954 for almost total abolition of restrictions to capital movements. The two main exceptions are as follows:

(a) The issuance of securities (bonds and shares) in national capital markets requires an authorization that is not granted automatically.

(b) The Dutch follow a rather restrictive policy toward the purchase by their residents of foreign securities or fixed assets.

INDEX